Scotsgate

Rhymes, Legends and Traditions

Edited by
Ian D. Hendry
Graham Stephen

Oliver & Boyd

Preface

It is our hope that readers of SCOTSGATE, young and old alike, may pass through a literary gateway to enjoy this selection of prose, poetry and traditional material, drawn from the rich storehouse of Scottish Literature.

SCOTSGATE is intended to be a companion volume to SCOTSCAPE, and in a similar vein we have concentrated on producing a wide variety of prose, poem and song. As much of the literary tradition of Scotland is closely connected with particular environments, we have chosen to present our selection in a series of themes reflecting the subject content.

As the re-awakening of public interest in written material in Scots continues to flourish, we hope that SCOTSGATE may play a small part in fostering and developing this interest in and appreciation of all aspects of Scottish writing.

IAN D HENDRY

GRAHAM STEPHEN

Illustrations by Shirley Tourret

Oliver & Boyd
Robert Stevenson House
1–3 Baxter's Place
Leith Walk
Edinburgh EH1 3BB

A Division of Longman Group Ltd

ISBN 0 05 003374 3

Printed in Singapore by
Tien Mah Litho Printing Co (Pte) Ltd.

Contents

Origins of Some of the Items in this Book

December Day, Hoy Sound

A Lullaby

Orcadian Lullaby

Skye Boat Song

The Seven Taps o'Bennachie

Fa's Feel are Ye?

Donald Dinnie

The Flit

Silver City

Glencoe

Coo'ters Candy

The Kelpie's Curse

Yellow-Haired Laddie

The Famous Tay Whale

Parents' Lines and Visits

Where is the Glasgow

Black Tom's Dream

Ibrox

Glasgow Street

The Winds of Edinburgh

The Bursting Boughs of May

Ballad, Song and Rhyme

Canedolia: an off-concrete scotch fantasia

oa! hoy! awe! ba! mey!

who saw?
rhu saw rum. garve saw smoo. nigg saw tain. lairg saw lagg.
rigg saw eigg. largs saw haggs. tongue saw luss. mull saw yell.
stoer saw strone. drem saw muck. gask saw noss. unst saw cults.
echt saw banff. weem saw wick. trool saw twatt.

how far?
from largo to lunga from joppa to skibo from ratho to shona from
ulva to minto from tinto to tolsta from soutra to marsco from
braco to barra from alva to stobo from fogo to fada from gigha to
gogo from kelso to stroma from hirta to spango.

what is it like there?
och it's freuchie, it's faifley, it's wamphray, it's frandy, it's
sliddery.

what do you do?
we foindle and fungle, we bonkle and meigle and maxpoffle. we
scotstarvit, armit, wormit, and even whifflet. we play at crosstobs,
leuchars, gorbals, and finfan. we scavaig, and there's aye a bit of
tilquhilly. if it's wet, treshnish and mishnish.

what is the best of the country?
blinkbonny! airgold! thundergay!

and the worst?
scrishven, shiskine, scrabster, and snizort.

listen! what's that?
catacol and wauchope, never heed them

tell us about last night
well, we had a wee ferintosh and we lay on the quiraing. it was
pure strontian!

but who was there?
petermoidart and craigenkenneth and cambusputtock and
ecclemuchty and corriehulish and balladolly and altnacanny and
clauchanvrechan and stronachlochan and auchenlachar and
tighnacrankie and tilliebruaich and killieharra and invervannach
and achnatudlem and machrishellach and inchtamurchan and
auchterfechan and kinlochculter and ardnawhallie and invershuggle

and what was the toast?
schiehallion! schiehallion! schiehallion!

Edwin Morgan

Croodin' Doo

Oh, whaur hae ye been this live-long day
My little wee croodin' doo?
I've been tae see my step-mother
Mammy, oh mak ma bed noo

And what did your step-mother gie ye tae eat
My little wee croodin' doo?
She gied me but a wee wee fish
A' covered in green and blue

And what did ye dae wi the bones o your fish
My little wee croodin' doo?
I gied them tae my wee wee dog
Mammy, oh mak my bed noo

And what did your dog dae when he ate o the bones
My little wee croodin' doo?
He stretched his wee wee limbs and deid
Mammy as I hae do noo
Mammy as I hae do noo.

Skye Boat Song

Speed bonny boat like a bird on the wing
"Onward" the sailors cry
Carry the lad that was born to be King
Over the sea to Skye

Loud the winds howl, loud the waves roar
Thunder claps rend the air
Baffled our foes stand on the shore
Follow they will not dare

Though the waves leap, soft shall ye sleep
Ocean's a royal bed
Rocked in the deep Flora will keep
Watch by your weary head

Many's the lad fought on that day
Well the claymore could wield
When the night came, silently lay
Dead on Culloden's field

Burned are our homes, exile and death
Scatter the loyal men,
Yet e'er the sword cool in the sheath
Charlie will come again

Fine Flowers in the Valley

She sat doon below a thorn
Fine Flowers in the valley
An' there she has her sweet babe born
And the green leaves they grow rarely

"Smile na sae sweet, my bonnie babe,"
Fine flowers in the valley,
"An' ye smile sae sweet, ye'll smile me deid."
And the green leaves they grow rarely.

She's ta'en oot her little pen-knife,
And twinn'd the sweet babe o' its life.

She's howket a grave by the light o' the moon,
And there she's buried her sweet babe in.

As she was going to the church,
She saw a sweet babe in the porch.

"O sweet babe, an' thou were mine,
I wad cleed thee in the silk sae fine."

"O mither dear, when I was thine,
Ye didna prove tae me sae kind."

The Bonny Boy

Oh, father, dear father, pray what is this ye've done
You have wed me to a college boy
A boy it's far too young
For he is only sixteen years and I am twenty one
He's my bonny bonny boy and he's growin

For we were going through college
When some boys were playing ball
When there I saw my own true love
The fairest of them all
When there I saw my own true love
The fairest of them all
He's my bonny bonny boy and he's growin

For at the age of sixteen years
He was a married man
And at the age of seventeen
The father of a son
And at the age of twenty-one
He did become a man
But the green grass o'er his grave it was growin

I will buy my love some flannel
And I'll make my love a shroud
With every stitch I put in it
The tears they will flow down
With every stitch I put in it
The tears they will flow down
And the green grass o'er his grave it is growin

The Yellow-Haired Laddie

The maidens are smiling in rocky Glencoe
The clansmen are aiming to rush the foe
Gay banners are streaming as forth leads the clan
And the yellow-haired laddie is first in the van.

The pibroch is kindling their hearts in the war
Cameron slogan is heard from afar
They close for the struggle where many shall fall
But the yellow-haired laddie is foremost of all.

He towers on the wave like the wild rolling tide
No kinsmen of Evans' shall stand by his side
The Camerons gather around him alone
He heeds not the danger, and fear is unknown.

The plumes of his bonnet are seen in the fight
The beacons of valour they light with the sight
But he saw not yon claymore, a traitrous thrust –
And the plumes and his bonnet were laid in the dust.

The maidens are smiling in rocky Glencoe
The clansmen approach, they have vanquished the foe
But sudden the cheeks of the maidens grew pale
For the sound of the coronach comes on the gale.

The maidens are crying in rocky Glencoe
From warriors eyelids the bitter drops blow
Where, but oh, where is our chieftain so dear?
The yellow-haired laddie lies low on the brae.

The maidens are wailing in rocky Glencoe
There's gloom in the valley at sunrise will go
No sun can the gloom from our hearts chase away
For the yellow-haired laddie lies cauld in the clay.

Faraway Tom

When the calendar brings in the cuckoo
And the summer comes followin' on
Then the thin mists of day
See him runnin' away
And they know him as Faraway Tom

He sees the fox leavin' his hollow
And he knows where the badger is gone
And he watches the fawn
In the sheltering thorn
But they don't see old Faraway Tom

The earth is his bed and his pillow
And his sheets are the clothes he has on
He sleeps all afternoon
Then he's huntin' the moon
Till it rises for Faraway Tom

He knows nothing of letters nor learning
And of manners and such he has none
And he numbers the seasons
On fingers and toes
As they pass over Faraway Tom

But what of the winters to follow?
Will age and cold winds bring him down?
Oh, where will he lie
When the snow fills the sky
And the years tell on Faraway Tom

When the calendar . . .

Dave Goulder

Where is the Glasgow?

Oh, where is the Glasgow where I used tae stey,
The white wally closes done up wi' pipe cley:
Where ye knew every neighbour frae first floor tae third,
And tae keep your door locked was considered absurd;
Do you know the folk steying next door tae you?

And where is the wee shop where I used tae buy.
A quarter o'totties, a tuppeny pie,
A bag o'broken biscuits an' three totty scones,
An' the wumman aye asked, 'How's your maw gettin' on?'
Can your big supermarket give service like that?

And where is the tram-car that once did the ton
Up the Great Western Road on the old Yoker run?
The conductress aye knew how to deal wi' a nyaff –
'If ye're gaun,then get oan, if ye're no, then get aff!'
Are there ony like her on the buses the day?

The Scaffie Song

There's dustmen and bucketmen
And binmen they're the same
Refuse collectors is just another name
In toons and in villages
Wherever is your hame,
You a' need the work o' the scaffie.

Chorus
If it wisnae for the scaffies
What would we dae
The streets would be polluted wi'
Rats and rubbish tae
The litter bins would pile up high
And higher every day
If it wisnae for the work o' the scaffies.

Bins, bags and buckets
Are heaped in the street
Wi' tattie-peelings, plastics
And tins frae food we eat,
Early morning, just like magic,
It's a' disappeared –
Thanks tae the work o' the scaffies.

Chorus
If it wisnae for the scaffies
What would we dae
The streets would be polluted wi'
Rats and rubbish tae
The litter bins would pile up high
And higher every day
If it wisnae for the work o' the scaffies.

Mary Kellagher

Farewell to Tarwathie

Farewell to Tarwathie, adieu, Mormond Hill
And the dear land of Crimond, I bid ye farewell;
I'm bound out for Greenland and ready to sail
In hopes to find riches in hunting the whale

Adieu to my comrades, for a while we must pairt
And likewise the dear lass wha fair won my hairt;
The cold ice of Greenland my love will not chill
And the longer my absence more loving she'll feel

Our ship is weel rigged and she's ready to sail
Our crew they are anxious to follow the whale;
Where the icebergs do float and the stormy winds blaw
Where the land and the ocean are covered wi' snaw

The cold coast of Greenland is barren and bare
No seed-time or harvest is ever known there;
And the birds here sing sweetly on mountain and dale
But there isnae a birdie to sing to the whale

There is no habitation for a man to live there
And the King of that country is the fierce Greenland bear;
And there'll be no temptation to tarry long there
Wi' our ship bumper full we will homeward repair.

Oh, dear me, the mill is runnin' fast
And we, poor shifters, cannie get nae rest
Shiftin' bobbins, coarse and fine
They fairly mak' ye work for your 10/9d.

Oh, dear me, I wish the day was done
Runnin' up and doon the pass is nae fun
Shiftin' piece and sparin' warp, weft and twine
There's no much pleasure livin' off o' 10/9.

Oh, dear me, the world is ill-divided
Them that works the hardest, are the least provided
But I must lie contented, dark days or fine
To feed and clothe my bairnies off o' 10/9.

The Lord's Prayer

This rendering in old Scots is quoted by John Pinkerton in his
History of Scotland (1797).

Oor fader quhilk beest i Hevin.
Hallowit weird thyne nam.
Cum thyne kinrik.
Be dune thyne wull as is i Hevin, sva po yerd.
Oor dailie breid gif us thilk day.
And forleit us uor skaths, as we forleit tham
quha skath us. And leed us na intil temtation.
Butan fre us fra evil. Amen.

The 23rd Psalm in Scots

The Lord is my Shepherd; in nocht am I wantin',
In the haughs o' green girse does He mak me lie doon;
While mony puir straiglers are bleatin' and pantin',
By saft-flowin' burnies He leads me at noon.

When aince I had strayed far awa in the bracken,
And daidled till gloamin' cam ower a' the hills;
Nae dribble o' water my sair drooth to slacken
And dark grow'd the nicht wi' its haars and its chills.

Awa frae the fauld, strayin' fit-sair and weary,
I thocht I had naethin' to dae but to dee.
He socht me and fand me in mountain hechts dreary
He gangs by fell paths which He kens best for me.

And noo, for His name's sake, I'm dune wi' a' fearin',
Though cloods may aft gaither and soughin' win's blaw.
"Hoo this?" or "Hoo that?" – oh, prevent me frae speirin';
His will is aye best, and I daurna say Na.

The valley o' death winna fleg me to thread it
Though awfu' the darkness, I weel can foresee;
Wi' His rod and His staff He wull help me to tread it
Then wull its shadows, saw gruesome, a' flee.

Forfochen in presence o' foes that surround me,
My Shepherd a table wi' denties has spread;
The Thyme and the Myrtle blaw fragrant aroond me —
He brims a fu' cup and poors oil on my head.

Surely guidness an' mercy, despite a' my roamin',
Wull gang wi' me doon to the brink o' the river,
Ayont it nae mair o' the eerie and gloamin',
I wull bide in the Hame o' my Faither for ever.

The Twenty-Third Pschalme

This, the best-loved of the Psalms, was thus beautifully paraphased by
Alexander Montgomerie, who was in the service of Regent Morton and
James VI, and in his devout old age published all the Psalms in metrical form.

The Lord maist hie
I know will be
An herd to me;.
I cannot lang have stress, nor stand in neid;
He makes my lair
In fields maist fair,
Quhair I bot care,
Reposing at my pleasure, safety feid.

He sweetly me convoys,
Quhair naething me annoys,
But pleasure brings.
He brings my mynd
Fit to sic kynd,
That foes, or fears of foe cannot me grieve.
He does me leid
In perfect freid,
And for his name he never will me lieve.

Thoch I wald stray,
Ilk day by day,
In deidly way,
Yet will I not dispair; I fear none ill,
For quhy thy grace
In every place,
Does me embrace,
Thy rod and shepherd's crook me comfort still,
In spite of foes
My tabil grows,
Thou balms my head with joy;
My cup owerflows.

Kyndness and grace,
Mercy and peice,
Sall follow me for all my wretched days,
And me convoy,
To endless joy,
In heaven quhair I sall be with thee always.

Legend and Fable

Black Tom's 'Dream'

On the site where Gillespie Hospital used to stand, formerly stood an ancient mansion that some years after the conclusion of the American War of Independence, was used by Lieutenant-General Robertson of Lawers, who had served through the whole of the war, as his town residence. The General, on his return to Europe, brought with him a negro called 'Black Tom,' who remained in his service as a servant. Tom's own particular room was on the ground floor of the house, and he was frequently heard to complain that he could not rest in it, for every night the figure of a headless woman, carrying a child in her arms, rose up from the hearth and frightened him terribly.

No one paid much attention to poor Tom's troubles, as they thought they were caused by dreams caused by over-indulgence, as the negro's character for sobriety was not very remarkable. But a strange thing happened when the General's old residence was pulled down to make way for James Gillespie's Hospital. There under the hearthstone which had caused 'Black Tom' so many restless nights, was discovered a box containing the body of a woman, from which the head had been severed, and beside her lay the remains of an infant, wrapt in a pillow-case trimmed with lace. The unfortunate lady appeared to have been murdered without any warning; she was fully dressed, and her scissors were yet hanging by a ribbon to her side, and her thimble was also in the box, having apparently dropped from the shrivelled finger of the corpse!

From *The Haunted Homes and Family Legends of Great Britain*
by John H. Ingram

The Last of the Picts

Long, long ago, there were folk in this country called the Picts. Wee short men they were, with red hair, long arms, and feet so broad that when it rained they could turn them up over their heads for umbrellas.

The Picts were great folk for the ale they brewed from the heather. Many wanted to know how they made it, but the Picts would not give away the secret, handing it down from one to the other.

Then the Picts were at war with the rest of the country, and many of them were killed. Soon only a handful of them were left, and they fought a great battle with the Scots. They lost the battle, and all but two of them were killed. These two were father and son.

The King of the Scots had these men brought before him, to frighten them into telling him the secret of the heather ale. He told them that if they did not reveal the secret, he must torture them.

"Well," said the older man to the King, "I see it is useless to resist. But one condition you must agree before you learn the secret".

"What is that?" said the King.

"Will you fulfil it if it does not harm you?"

"I will," said the King, "and promise to do so."

"Then," said the Pict,

> "My son you must kill
> Ere I will tell
> How we brew the yill
> From the heather bell!"

The King was astonished, but he ordered the lad to be put to death immediately.

When the Pict saw his son was dead, he stood up before the King and cried:

"Now do what you like with me. You might have forced my son, for he's but a weak lad, but you'll not force me.

> "And though you may me kill,
> I'll not you tell
> How we brew yill
> From the heather bell."

The King was very angry. He had been outwitted by a wild man of the hills. It was useless to kill the Pict, so he was thrown into prison.

And there he lived until he was an old, old man, bedridden and blind. Everyone had forgotten him, then one night some lads sharing his prison cell boasted about their feats of strength. The old Pict leaned out of bed and stretched out his hand.

"Let me feel your wrists," he said. "I want to compare them with the arms of the Picts."

Just for fun, the lads held out a thick iron bar for him to feel. The old Pict grasped the bar between his fingers and thumb, gave it a twist and snapped it in two, as though it was the stem of a clay-pipe.

"It's rather gristly," he said, "but the wrists of the Picts were much harder and stronger!"

From *The Well at the World's End*
by Norah and William Montgomerie

18

The Goodwife of Kettock's Mills

On the banks of the Aberdeenshire Don, near the Brig o' Balgownie, once stood Kettock's Mills. Kettock's Mills and "millers" must have served many generations of the Oldmachar parishioners to grind their "meldruns" of oatmeal in the long past. Like the lichens which cling to the rocky banks of the river, there clings to Kettock's Mills a grim folk-story of the olden time, such as might easily have formed the subject of a ballad in our early literature.

The miller's wife died, we are told, "despite the best medical advice". And — whether by deliberate decision of the deceased's relatives, or by sheer overlook to their part — she was buried in the Churchyard of the adjacent Cathedral, with a valuable ring on one of her fingers. Naturally, some one had observed the omission to remove the ring, and it became known in the neighbourhood that the ring had gone to the grave with the dead lady.

Now, in every age, it has been reckoned a good trait in the Scots character to dislike anything being "connacht"! Perhaps an excess of that virtue — why call it avarice? — had impelled the thrifty local Sexton to correct such prodigal waste. At any rate, at midnight of the burial day, armed with his familiar mattock and spade, the Sexton returned to his haunts among the tombs outside the walls of the sacred old minster. He re-opened the new-made grave, lifted the coffin lid, and decided to cut the ring off the corpse's finger. The first touch of the knife, however, produced a miraculous effect. The "corpse" came back to life again! "Aliss!" she cried. And again: "Help me up!" One can well imagine the predicament in which the ghoulish Sexton found himself at the moment. The poor woman had been buried alive! Thoughts of concealing his identity must have followed upon the first throes of the Sexton's terror. Whether he stayed to help, or instantly fled, we are not told. But the unhappy miller's wife got up from her "narrow bed," walked home in her winding-sheet, and knocked vigorously at the door of her earthly home. Aroused by the din she made, her husband got out of bed, and as he groped his way to "answer the door", was heard to say: "Gin my wife warna deid, I'd say that was her knock!" Before opening the door he called

19

out: "Wha's there?" Back came the reply: "Jist yer ain wife! Lat's in it's caul'!" On the door being opened, the unfortunate lady, clad in her ghostly burial garments, walked into the house! A veil must be drawn over this extraordinary re-union of the Miller and his Wife.

The reader is left to content himself with the assurance — given in the story — that thereafter the worthy pair lived together for many happy years, and that the goodwife of Kettock's Mills, who had been buried as dead, returned to life to bear several sturdy children. So the Sexton's unsavoury midnight adventure was touched with good, in that it was the means of saving a soul alive!

From *In and Around the Aulton*
by William Skea

Legend of the White Heather

There once lived a laird who had a great estate and he was dearly loved and respected by his own people, the villagers and his workers. He only had one fault — he didn't believe in good luck and wasn't superstitious in any way. And when they went on a hunt, a boar hunt or a deer hunt, all the women of the village would come out and meet the huntsmen and offer them good luck charms to protect them from getting attacked by a wild boar or falling off their horses or something. But the laird would just laugh and scorn them, call them "children"! Because he never believed in good luck or bad luck or anything like that. And the thing was, he was the finest hunter among them all, he always came off best at the hunt. And he never carried any lucky charms of any description, which was a great thing in these days.

Till one day he was going on another hunt, a boar hunt. As usual the ladies came and offered their men charms which they accepted. This old woman, the oldest woman of the village, came to the laird.

She says, "Why don't you take something with you, sir, to bring you luck?"

He says, "Old woman, I don't need anything to bring me luck. I've never needed anything in all my days and I don't think I'll need it now! I don't believe in these things."

She says, "Take a good luck charm with you, sir! You'll probably need it."

"Not me," he said to the old woman, "I never bother about these things."

So they set on their way on the hunt, all the huntsmen with their hounds to hunt the boar. And after they had gone a long way there rose a great black boar. And they all set after it.

But the laird got lost. He landed by himself. And he got on the track of the boar till he got it cornered. It charged his horse and his horse reared up and the laird fell off. He was right on the face of a cliff, a steep cliff with a drop of hundreds of feet. And when his horse reared up he rolled — he went right over the face of the cliff and he fell for about twenty or thirty feet.

He's trying to get any kind of stone or something to grip, when he grips this bush, a large bush. He hung on to it. And it took his weight. He started to shout for help. He must have hung on for at least half an hour. He was afraid the bush was going to give way from the face of the cliff. But it still took his weight.

And some of the men heard him shouting. They came to the face of the cliff, and lowered down ropes and rescued him.

When he came up he was all frightened and shaking.

He said, "I thought my time had come! If it wasn't for that bush that saved my life I would have plunged right over the cliff!"

And one of the men said, "Sir, that wasn't a bush. That was a sod of heather!"

So he told one of the men, "Well, you go back down there and bring me up a piece of that heather — it saved my life! Because I want to take it home with me."

And the man was lowered down with a rope. He took a sod of the heather and brought it up. And when he brought it up to the laird it was white, white heather.

So the laird fetched it back to his castle and told the gardener he wanted it put right at his front door. And the next morning everyone came and admired the laird's white heather at the front of his mansion. They were thankful for it, that it had saved their master's life.

Each year it spread and got bigger till he was able to give everyone a piece of it, everyone got a piece of that heather and kept it. And they gave it to somebody else. The luck of the white heather spread far and wide, till today it's spread over three parts of the world.

From the oral narration of Duncan Williamson

The Kelpie's Curse

Fae ghoulies an' ghosties and lang-legged beasties
And things that go bump in the nicht,
Good Lord deliver us.

And that most certainly included kelpies, the fearsome, form-changing water-horses which haunted Scotland's rivers in the olden times. Many are the strange tales of fates befallen by solitary travellers, frightened, wounded or even devoured by kelpies. But one strange tale tells of a man who broke a kelpie — as one would break a wild horse — by putting a bridle on the creature and subduing it to his will. This daring man was Graham, Laird of Morphie, near Montrose, who then used the creature to drag stones from the River North Esk to build his new castle. On its completion he released the kelpie, which before disappearing into the river, cursed him and his line — a curse which strange to tell was to hold meaning for the Grahams of Morphie, for misfortune was to dog this family until the line was ended.

In the nineteenth century, a local poet George Beattie, wrote a poetical work entitled John o' Arnha', in which the drunken hero while homeward bound along the banks of the North Esk meets and causes offence to an old woman. The old hag is really a witch and she exacts her revenge by cursing him roundly and bringing him face to face with the Morphie Kelpie. . . .

John row'd owr dykes, and lair'd in
  ditches,
Mutterin' malisons on witches;
Neist owr the plain, and down a hill,
He heard the clackin' of a mill:
Again the spunkie's waverin' light
Discovert to his wildert sight,
In boiling wrath, the North-esk stream
Thuddin onward, white wi' feam.
He heard a voice, wi' muckle dool,
Croonin' i' the Ponnage-pool;
An' this it said, or seemed to say,
'Ah, willawins! alack for aye!
O sair's my back, an' sair my banes,
Leadin' the Laird o' Marphie's stanes;
The Laird o' Marphie canna thrive
As lang's the Kelpie is alive.'
The thunder growl'd in lower tone,
As if to let the voice get on.
'God help ye! be ye friend or fae,'
Quo' John,' it's wrang to use ye sae;
To me your griefs ye needna tell,
For, waes my heart, I'm waur mysel.'
When, by the lightning's glare, he saw
A sight surpassing nature's law.
A stalwart monster, huge in size,
Did streight frae out the river rise;
Behind a dragon's tail he wore,
Twa bullock's horns stack out before;
His legs were horn, wi' joints o' steel,
His body like the crocodile.
On smellin' John, he gae a scoil,
Then plung's and gar'd the water boil
Anon he stood upo' the shore,
And did for vengeance loudly roar.

...The Kelpie's Curse

Sair back and sair banes
Drivin' the Laird o' Marphies stanes.
The Laird o' Marphie'll never thrive
As lang as the kelpie is alive

From *John o' Arnha'*
by George Beattie

Weather-Wise and Country Lore

Lammas, Lammas
At eleveen oors
Farewell summer
And a' the flooers

Sweetie wifie, sweetie wifie,
Ding doon snaw!
Ding doon a hunner,
And I'll catch them a'.

Rainy, rainy, rattlestanes
Dinna rain on me:
Rain on John O'Groats hoose
Faur owre the sea.

The rhymes above were often sung by children to mark a change in the weather or season.

It was said among the old people that if they took note of which direction the wind was blowing on Hogmanay, the last night of the year, that would be its prevailing direction throughout the year to come. They had a rhyme about it which went like this:

> South wind on Hogmanay, heat and fruitfulness;
> West wind on Hogmanay, fish to craig;
> North wind on Hogmanay, cold and flaying;
> East wind on Hogmanay, fruit on trees.

The freakish uncertainty of our climate, the deceptiveness of spring when the sun shines gaily one day and the next one may be as cold again as winter, has made wise ones warn the coming generation to

> Ne'er cast a clout
> Till May be out.

When snow falls the Scottish child is told it is Norroway witches shaking their feathers.

There are many prophecies regarding weather taken from local signs — for example, hills which wear a cowl bring rain to the plains.

> When Falkland Hill puts on a cap
> The Howe o' Fife will get a drap

say the folk of Fife, and in Annandale they have noted that

> When Criffel wears a hap
> Skiddaw wats full well o' that.

"Many haws, many snaws" the old folks say, when they see the thorn white with blossom, believing that a forseeing Providence will supply more food if a hard winter is to set in.

Candlemas ended the forty days of Yule. This being a Quarter Day, the signs were carefully observed.

> Candlemas Day, gin ye be fair,
> The half o' winter's to come and mair;
> Candlemas Day, gin ye be foul
> The half o' winter's gane at Yule.

Another rhyme runs:

> Gin Candlemas be fair and clear
> There'll be twa winters in the year.
>> If the lavero sings afore Candlemas,
>> She'll greet twice as lang eftir!

A Januar haddock
A Februar bannock
And a March pint o' ale

Thun'er in May
Hunger for aye.
Thun'er in June
Pits a' thing in tune.

A January spring
Is worth naething

Mist in May, and heat in June.
Maks the harvest richt sune.

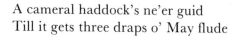

A Merse mist alang the Tweed
In a harvest mornin's gude indeed.

A cameral haddock's ne'er guid
Till it gets three draps o' May flude

February, if ye be fair,
The sheep will mend and nothing mair;
February, if ye be foul,
The sheep will die in every pool.

March brings the lammie
And buds the thorn,
But blows through the flint
Of an ox's horn.

A wet May and a windy
Maks a full barnyard and a findy.

Findy (or *finnie*), a Galloway word, here means that the grain has a
good feeling in the hand.

THE WEATHERLORE OF DUNCAN WILLIAMSON

If March comes in bright and clear
There'll be two winters in the year.

Folk in olden days very rarely made a mistake in forecasting the weather because they could read nature. And they learned from nature how to read the weather.

If you see the sheep gathering on the knowe and the sheep starting to dance, there's heavy gales coming.

Early stars (before it's dark) are a sign of really heavy frost to come, and a long time of frost.

If water lies level on furrows in a ploughed field, there's more rain to come.

Leaves falling straight down from the trees are a sign of good weather coming; if they fall at an angle, there's more gales and bad weather to come.

When tested with the finger, the spikes on the thorns on bushes, if sharp, a long good autumn is coming; if blunt, winter is coming soon.

If the white hares or the stoats turn white earlier than usual (the end of October), a hard winter is ahead.

If the birds start mating early, spring will be early (mid-February or so) — "an early nest is a guid sign".

If the bushes are loaded with fruit, with plenty of hips and haws, and the trees have a large crop of berries — rowan and elderberry — then it will be a hard winter right through: nature is providing a supply for the birds.

If the berries are very scarce, it will be a mild winter: the birds won't be needing many berries because they'll get other feeding during the winter.

If you see the cattle in the fields putting on their coats of hair early and the horses' coats are coming on earlier than usual, this is a sign winter is coming fast. Winter will be early for the animals' coats are needed to see them through the winter.

Insects flying low — two or three feet above your head — is a sign that it will rain for a long period (moisture in the air won't rise if the air is too wet high up).

If there are no insects flying within sight — if the swallows fly up after them — then there will be a nice dry spell.

An owl hooting in daylight signals rain, a long spell of rain: owls hate rain.

A dew drop hanging too long (a couple of hours) on a blade of grass or on a wire fence without falling off signals a dull, dull day — probably going to be rain.

If you see gulls taking off from the shores and making for the mainland, the fields — it's going to be stormy.

Gulls dancing on the earth signals a dry spell. When gulls pat the earth they are hunting for worms which are well down in the earth. The gulls are "kidding-on" it's raining with their feet to make the worms think it's raindrops — the worms will come up for the gulls to eat. A worm has to go down deep when the earth gets dry, for a worm can't survive without moisture.

When the moss on the bark of the trees grows faster on one side than on the other, it will be a stormy winter. With the mosses growing on the sheltered sides of the trees faster than on the fronts of the trees, the wee birds — the tree creepers — will keep to the one side feeding on the insects which feed only on the mosses. Thus if you see the tree-creepers creeping straight up the tree (keeping to the one side), it will be a hard winter.

When birds start to feed and gather together in wee flocks and fight over what they are getting, there's going to be snow: the birds are preparing for the snow.

If you come across many rabbit nests in a hollow, this signals a long dry summer. A bird won't build a nest or a rabbit make a burrow in a hollow if it's going to be flooded or washed out, for his young ones would be drowned when the nest filled with water.

If the crows make their nests in the thickest parts of the trees (for protection), it will be a stormy summer.

When you see a crow tearing down its old nest in early March it's a sign of a good summer: if he tears it down, he'll have plenty of time to build a new one — it'll be a good, long warm summer. You just need to walk in the woods and find the old sticks lying at the foot of the trees — he throws them out: it's going to be a great summer!

If you see the crows building on to their old nests, look out! It's going to be a very harsh summer, a lot of wind and rain. If the crow knows he only has a little time, he'll not tear the old nest down.

If you go to a brook or a burn where there's usually a lot of wee fish (minnans) or wee trout and they are gone, this is a sign of thunder. Trout hate thunder; they hide before it comes.

If you see the tops of the trees in a wood going forward and back too often, or the tops of the trees touching each other, these are signs of gales coming.

If you come to an anthill and the ants are gone — they're not busy but are away down in the hill — look out! It's going to be a bad spell of rain. Insects don't like to crawl in rain.

When the corn is shot, coming to pea, late, — it will be a bad spell; if it's early — it will be a good spell. The corn will shoot about the twelfth of July, about the middle of July. If the corn is not shot, there's no heads on it, by the end of July, then the autumn will be very bad. If the peas begin to show about the first of July, then there will be a great spell at the harvest.

If you see cats sitting sunning themselves, a good spell is coming.

A busy shrew means hard times ahead.

A happy grasshopper, one that makes plenty of noise and singing, means a warm summer.

If the oak comes out before the ash
The summer will be one long splash;
But if the ash comes out before the oak,
You'll have no fear of getting a soak.

From the oral narration of Duncan Williamson

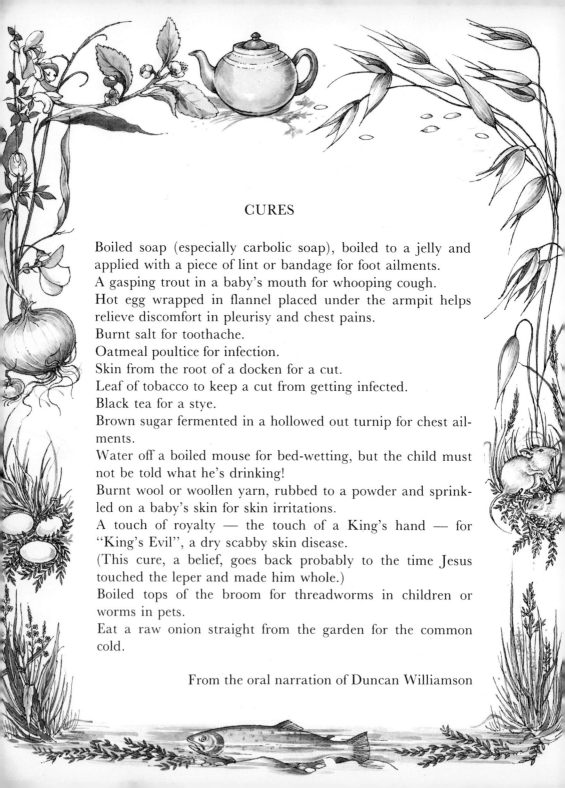

CURES

Boiled soap (especially carbolic soap), boiled to a jelly and applied with a piece of lint or bandage for foot ailments.

A gasping trout in a baby's mouth for whooping cough.

Hot egg wrapped in flannel placed under the armpit helps relieve discomfort in pleurisy and chest pains.

Burnt salt for toothache.

Oatmeal poultice for infection.

Skin from the root of a docken for a cut.

Leaf of tobacco to keep a cut from getting infected.

Black tea for a stye.

Brown sugar fermented in a hollowed out turnip for chest ailments.

Water off a boiled mouse for bed-wetting, but the child must not be told what he's drinking!

Burnt wool or woollen yarn, rubbed to a powder and sprinkled on a baby's skin for skin irritations.

A touch of royalty — the touch of a King's hand — for "King's Evil", a dry scabby skin disease.

(This cure, a belief, goes back probably to the time Jesus touched the leper and made him whole.)

Boiled tops of the broom for threadworms in children or worms in pets.

Eat a raw onion straight from the garden for the common cold.

From the oral narration of Duncan Williamson

Granny's Knee

This was recited to the bairn who was being jigged up and down on the knee.

> This is the way the ladies ride
> Trit, trot, trit, trot, trit, trot:
> This is the way the gentlemen ride,
> Trit-trot, trit-trot, trit-trot, trit-trot:
> This is the way the cadgers ride
> Creels an' a', creels an' a'.

Another jingle to amuse the very young, with appropriate movement of the fingers.

> The doggie gaed tae the mill,
> This gait an that gait,
> A lick oot this wife's pokie,
> An' a lick oot that wife's pokie,
> A lop o the leid,
> A bit o the breid,
> An hame, loupie fer spang, loupie fer spang.

FACE RHYMES

Rhymes which bring into play a child's brow, eyes, nose and mouth.

There war a littel wee man
An he cam owre the hill   (*Mother 'walks' two fingers over brow*)
An he knock't at the dor   (*raps on brow with knuckles*)
An he keekit in   (*pokes forefinger towards eye*)
An he liftit the snek   (*grips nose and lifts gently*)
An he wypit his feet   (*wipes forefinger on upper lip*)
An he walk't in, walk't in, walk't in.   (*puts forefinger in open mouth.*)

Clap, clap handies
Mammy's awa tee wall;
Daddy's awa workin'
For a new shawl

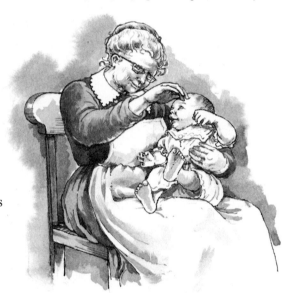

Johnnie Norie
Gaed up twa stappies
And in at the doorie.

Face Game

Here sits the King   (*brow*)
Here sits his men   (*eyes*)
Here sits the cock   (*right cheek*)
Here sits the hen   (*left cheek*)
Here sits the wee chickens   (*nose*)
Here they run in   (*mouth*)
Chinchopper, chinchopper   (*chin*)
Chinchopper, chin

Chin chappie,
Mou'merry,
Nose nappie,
Cheek cherry,
E'e winkie,
Broo brinkie,
Ower the hills and awa'

FINGER GAMES FROM DUNCAN WILLIAMSON

For two persons

> Put your finger in the craw's nest —
> The craw's no' in;
> The craw's at the back door
> Peckin' at a pin!

First person makes the craw's nest — a square with the first and second fingers of both hands.

First person says to second person, "Put your finger in the craw's nest — the craw's no' in." The second person pokes a finger down into the 'nest' believing the craw's no' in.

The first person then nips the second person's finger with the left thumb — the 'craw hiding at the bottom of the nest' — saying, "The craw's at the back door peckin' at a pin!"

For three persons

> This is the fox and the fox is asleep;
> When the fox is asleep he wriggles his feet —
> First the forefoot, then the hind;
> Then a forefoot and a hind.
> Should you wake the foxie up
> You will get a rap with the houndsman's whip!'

Leader and two or three children sit around a table. Leader holds a pencil or a stick in one hand and recites the verse with the accompanying finger motion.

For line one, hold up the thumb of one hand, "This is the fox." Then, while placing the hand on the table with all fingers extended and thumb pressed tightly in besides the first finger, say, "and the fox is asleep".

For the third and fourth lines of the verse the fingers are the fox's feet and the "wriggling" is done as follows: move the first finger, the little finger, the second finger and the third finger up and down respectively.

If anyone should move a thumb or wriggle the wrong "foot" at the wrong time, then the leader raps the fingers with the "whip" (the pencil or stick).

Each person takes a turn as houndsman (leader).

For two or more persons

> This is the lady's looking glass;
> This is the baby's cradle;
> This is the roadman's sweeping brush;
> This is the lady's ladle!

Leader recites verse with this accompanying finger motion.

First, interlock hands with fingers pointing downwards. With hands folded tightly closed, raise the two little fingers saying, "This is the lady's looking glass." Then, raising the two thumbs, say, "This is the baby's cradle." Then, raising only the first finger closest to the thumbs and without moving the rest of the fingers, say, "This is the roadman's sweeping brush". And raising the third finger of the opposite hand to that of the raised first finger — if you can! — say, "This is the lady's ladle!"

For two or more persons

> I want to build myself a stack;
> I build and I build and I build like that;
> I build and I build and I build so high —
> It fell down on a passerby!

Facing one another in sitting position, two (or more) persons build a 'stack' by piling up their closed fists. First person alternates left and right fists with second person's fists. 'Building' is done by shifting the fist on the bottom of the stack to the top. First person recites the verse — corresponding scansion to building. When fists are reached as high as possible (by the end of the verse) they are tumbled down — the 'stack' falling.

For two persons

> This is the one who broke the barn;
> This is the one who stole the corn;
> This is the one who ran awa';
> This is the one who told on a';
> And wee peerie pinkie paid them all!

First person holds out a hand with fingers and thumb extended. Second person, with thumb and first finger of one hand, grabs each finger of first person's hand — progressing from thumb to little finger, reciting each line of the verse respectively.

For two or more persons

> This is the way the teacher stands;
> This is the way she holds her hands;
> This is the way she bends her knees,
> And this is the way she dances.

Leader holds out both hands to others, and recites the verse, showing the way the fingers must move. The others are to follow the leader's finger movements with their own fingers. The leader must watch to see they make no mistakes. Whoever makes a mistake is "out". The last one becomes the new leader.

Finger movements:

Close hands into fists.
Leader says, "This is the way the teacher stands," and raises first fingers of both hands.
Leader says, "This is the way she holds her hands," and raises all fingers on both hands.
Leader says, "This is the way she bends her knees," and keeping all fingers up, only the second fingers of both hands are bent down.

Leader says, "And this is the way she dances." With second fingers still bent down and with all other fingers and thumbs still up, only the third fingers of both hands must be jiggled up and down — "she dances" [not so easy!].

From the oral narration of Duncan Williamson

FINGER COUNTS

A finger play beginning with the little finger, in which each finger is shaken rapidly in turn.

Dance, my wee man, ringman, midman, foreman
Dance, dance forthoomiken, canna weel dance his lane

A finger count beginning with the thumb.

Thumb bold,
Thibity-thold,
Langman,
Lickpan,
Mamma's little man.

In Orkney, the grannies would delight the young children by teaching them names of the fingers which would vary from island to island. On North Ronaldsay the children would be taught:

Peedie, Peedie   (little finger)
Paddy Luddy   (third finger)
Lady Whisle   (middle finger)
Lodey Whusle   (index finger)
Great Odomonclod(thumb)

On Sanday: Peediman
Lickpot
Langman
Loomikin
Toomikin

FEET

'John Smith, fallow fine,
Can ye shoe this horse o' mine?'
'Yes, Sir, and that I can,
As weel as ony man!
There's a nail upon the tae,
To gar the pony speel the brae;
There's a nail upon the heel,
Tae gar the pony pace weel;
There's a nail, and there's a brod,
There's a horsie weel shod.'

The bare foot is patted according to the words of the rhyme.

A rhyme for working the feet as the child sits on the holders lap.

'Feetiken, feetiken.
When will ye gang?'
'When the nichts turn short
And the days turn lang
I'll toddle and gang, toddle and gang!'

LULLABIES AND FIRESIDE RHYMES

This lullaby would be sung to a sick child.

Cockie Bendie's lyin' *seik*   (*sick*)
Guess ye what'll mend him
Twenty kisses in a *cloot*   (*cloth*)
Lassie, will ye send them?

When dancing a bairn on her knee the mother might sing:

Cripple Dick upon a stick
Sandy on a *soo*   (*sow*)
Ride a mile to Berwick, John
To buy a *pund* o' *oo*   (*pound*)   (*wool*)

Coo'ters Candy

1 There
was a wee las-sie aw-fy thin, A bun-dle o' bones wrapped up in skin.
Now she's get-tin' a wee dou-ble chin, Wi eat-in' coo'-ters can-dy.
Al-ly bal-ly, al-ly bal-ly bee, Sit-tin' on your mam-my's knee.
Greet-in' for a- no-ther baw-bee To buy some coo'-ters can-dy.

2 Poor wee Annie's greetin' too,
What can her poor mammy do,
But gi'e them a penny between them two,
To buy some Coo'ters candy?

Chorus:
Ally bally, ally bally bee,
Sittin' on your mammy's knee
Greetin' for another bawbee
To buy some coo'ters candy.

3 'Mammy gi'es my banky doon,
Here's auld Coo'ter comin' roon',
Wi' his basket on his croon
An' sellin' Coo'ters candy.'
Chorus:

4 'Dinna you greet, my wee babby,
You know your daddy's gone to sea,
Earnin' pennies for you and me
To buy some Coo'ters candy.'
Chorus:

Orcadian Lullaby

Ba, ba, lammie noo,
Cuddle doon tae mammie;
Trowies canna tak thoo,
Hushie ba, lammie;
Me bonnie, peerie bird
Sleepin in me bosie.

Nursery Rhyme

There was a wee bit mousikie,
That lived in Gilberaty-O,
It couldno' get a bite o' cheese,
For cheatie pussy-catty-o.

It said unto the cheeseky,
'Oh fain would I be at ye-O,
If 'twere no' for the cruel claws
Of cheatie pussy-catty-o'.

Anonymous

A Lullaby

O saftly sleep, my bonnie bairn!
Rock'd on this breast o' mine;
The heart that beats sae sair within
Will not awaken thine.

Lie still, lie still, ye canker'd thoughts!
That such late watches keep;
An' if ye break the mother's heart,
Yet let the baby sleep.

Dry up, dry up, ye saut, saut tears.
Lest on my brain ye dreep;
An' break in silence, waefu' heart,
An' let my baby sleep.

A Lullaby from Shetland

Hurr, hurr dee noo, Hurr, hurr dee noo,
Noo faa dee ower, my lammie.
Hurr, hurr dee noo, Hurr, hurr dee noo,
Dere nane sall get my lammie.
Hurr dee, Hurr dee, Mammie sall keep dee,
Hurr dee, Hurr dee, Mammie is here.

The 'hurr dee, hurr dee' refers to
the whirr of the spinning wheel.

Cradle Sang

Fa' owre, fa' owre, my hinny,
There's monie a weary airt;
And nae end to the traikin,
For man has a hungry hert.

What wud ye hae for ferlie
And no ken the want o'mair ?
The sün for a gowdan aipple:
The müne for a siller pear.

William Soutar

Da Fetlar Lullaby

The words of this lullaby were written by Sinclair Shewan, who lived at Still in the first half of the twentieth century. His son Walter, was a highly talented boatbuilder.

Husha-baa Mam's peerie flooer;
Sleep o sleep come ta dee shon.
Mam sall watch dee ooer be ooer
Till dy boannie sleep is done.

    Till dy boannie sleep is done.
    Till dy boannie sleep is done,
    Mam sall watch dee ooer be ooer
    Till dy boannie sleep is done.

Bide, da Simmer days ir comin;
Dan we'll rin aboot da knowes,
See da bees aa fleein, hummin,
Peerie lambs an muckle yowes,

    Peerie lambs an muckle yowes,
    Peerie lambs an muckle yowes,
    See da bees aa fleein, hummin,
    Peerie lambs an muckle yowes.

Noo dan! Here comes Willie Winkie,
Baetin, baetin on his drum;
Playin on his plinkie-plinkie;
Rest an slumber shon 'ill come.

    Rest an slumber shon 'ill come,
    Rest an slumber shon 'ill come,
    Playin on his plinkie-plinkie;
    Rest an slumber shon 'ill come.

Clamjamfry

The Winds of Edinburgh

As this town is situated on the borders of the sea, and surrounded by hills of an immense height, the currents of air are carried down between them with a rapidity and a violence which nothing can resist. It has frequently been known, that in the New Town at Edinburgh three or four people have scarce been able to shut the door of the house; and it is a very common accident to hear of sedan chairs being overturned. . . .

At other times, the winds, instead of rushing down with impetuosity, whirl about in eddies, and become still more dreadful. On these occasions it is almost impossible to stir out of doors, as the dust and stones gathered up in these vortices not only prevent your seeing, but frequently cut your legs by the velocity with which they are driven. The Scotch have a peculiar appellation for this, 'The Stour'.

The chief scene where these winds exert their influence, is the New Bridge, which, by being thrown over a long valley that is open at both ends, and particularly from being ballustraded on each side, admits the wind in the most charming manner imaginable; and you receive it with the same force you would do, were it conveyed to you through a pair of bellows. It is far from unentertaining for a man to pass over this bridge on a tempestuous day. In walking over it this morning I had the pleasure of adjusting a lady's petticoats which had blown almost entirely over her head, and which prevented her disengaging herself from the situation she was in; but in charity to her distress, I concealed her charms from public view. One poor gentleman, who was rather too much engaged with the novelty of the objects before him, unfortunately forgot his own hat and wig, which were lifted up by an unpremidated puff, and carried entirely away.

From *Letters from Edinburgh* by Edward Topham

Cocky-nit, cocky-nit, a penny the bit!
This was the favourite cry of a well-known street vendor of late nineteenth-century Edinburgh, Cocoa-Nut Tam. This photograph, taken in 1888, shows Cocoa-Nut Tam selling his wares at his stance near Halkerston's Wynd.

December Day, Hoy Sound

The unfurled gull on the tide, and over the skerry
Unfurling waves, and slow unfurling wreckage
— The Sound today a burning sapphire bough
Fretted with mimic spring.

                  The creatures of earth
Have seasons and stations, under the quartered sun
Ploughshare and cornstalk, millwheel and grinning rags.
The December seed kneels at his frosty vigil,
Sword by his side for the long crusade to the light
In trumpeting March, with the legion of lamb and leaf.

The sea grinds his salt behind a riot of masks.

Today on Hoy Sound random blossoms unfurl
Of feather and rust, a harlequin spring.

                  Tommorrow
The wave will weep like a widow on the rock,
Or howl like Lear, or laugh like a green child.

                        George Mackay Brown

Glencoe

Along the road from Ballachulish where the River Coe pours into
Loch Leven is a comfortable little village which boasts the most
grotesque sign-post in the British Isles:

The Village of Glencoe
Scene of the Famous Massacre
Teas and Refreshments, Tobacco and Cigarettes

This statement relieves the feeling of gloom with which a traveller
approaches the scene of the clan massacre.

    Glencoe is awesome, it is stark, it is, like all the wild mountains
of Scotland, a lesson in humility. Man has never existed for it; it
is, at least in sunlight, not unfriendly so much as utterly oblivious

of humanity. A man suddenly shot up into the moon might gaze at the cold, remote mountains with much the same chilly awe that he looks at the Pass of Glencoe. Here is a landscape without mercy. So far as Glencoe is concerned the first germ of life has never struggled from the warm slime. It is still dreaming of geological convulsions. Glencoe in sunlight does not make a man shudder because it is beautiful. It rather encourages him to sit down and look at it for a long time, as you sit down in the sand and look at the Sphinx, wondering what he can see in the sky. Perhaps it is God. Glencoe has the same expression.

The worst road in Scotland winds its way through the solitude. The iron-grey mountains fret the sky on either hand. Half the pass is in sunlight; half in cold shadow. Tough grass and soggy bog-land fill the narrow valley. There is no sound but the running of icy water, brown with peat; no movement but the wind in the long grass and the slow wheeling of some sinister bird high over the hills.

It was in the depth of winter in the year 1691 that all the Highlands were required to take an oath of allegiance to William III before the year was out. Every clan took this oath but the Macdonalds of Glencoe. Old MacIan, their chief, held out until the last moment. But he saw how foolish it was — or perhaps the women told him; anyhow, the old man set off through the snowdrifts to swear loyalty before the magistrates at Fort William. When he got there he discovered that the oath should be taken before the sheriff at Inveraray. So the old man goes on through the hard weather. The passes are deep in snow, the wind is bitter, and he does not reach Inveraray until January 6th. He takes oath, and the sheriff tells the authorities at Edinburgh that the clan has fallen into line.

Now, the authorities in Edinburgh — and notably Sir John Dalrymple, Secretary of State — are anxious to stamp out the Macdonalds. They are Papists. They are Jacobites. They are thieves and robbers. It would be easier to rule the country were they exterminated. When the register goes to the Privy Council in Edinburgh the name of Macdonald of Glencoe is found to have been obliterated, and the clan is formally liable to punishment. Now Dalrymple had written to a friend in Scotland expressing his delight that the time of grace expired in the depth of winter, because, as he put it, 'that is the proper season to maul them, in the cold, long nights.' He wrote to the commander-in-chief in Scotland on January 11th, 'My Lord Argyle tells me that Glencoe hath not taken the oaths; at which I rejoice — it's a great work of charity to be exact in rooting out that damnable sect, the worst in all the Highlands.'

So fellow Scotsmen plan the great 'work of charity'.

At the beginning of February — four weeks after the old Macdonald had taken the oath — a detachment of a hundred and twenty men of the Earl of Argyle's regiment — all Campbells and hereditary enemies of the Macdonalds — set out from the garrison at Inverlochy under the command of Campbell of Glenlyon. This man is a relative by marriage of the old chief's. The troops march through the snows and into the valley, where they express friendship for their victims and are received with true Highland hospitality. So murderers and victims settle down together.

Every morning the commander calls at the humble house of the old chief and takes his draught of usquebaugh. In the evenings he plays at cards with the family; and all the time in his pocket is the

45

savage death-knell of the clan: 'You are to put all to the sword under seventy. You are to have a special care that the old fox and his son do on no account escape your hands. You're to secure all avenues, that none escape; this you are to put in execution at five o'clock precisely, and by that time, or very shortly after it, I'll strive to be at you with a stronger party. If I do not come to you at five, you are not to tarry for me, but to fall on..!

At five o'clock of the dark winter morning the signal is given and the foul massacre begins. In every little hut scattered throughout the glen the same awful treachery occurs: guest murders his host and host's family. Lieutenant Lindsay comes with his men to the chief's house. The old man gets out of bed to receive him and is shot dead as he dresses. His wife, shamefully treated by the soldiers, dies the next day. The whole glen echoes with the cries of the murdered and shots of the murderers. One family receive a volley of shot as they sit round the early morning fire.

When light comes to Glencoe the snow is bloody and the smoke of the burning houses is going up in the frosty air. Thirty-eight Macdonalds have been murdered.

Colonel Hamilton, commanding officer at Inverlochy, arrives at breakfast-time to see how the 'act of charity' has panned out. He finds one old man mourning over the bodies of the dead. A Campbell catches sight of him, levels his flintlock and shoots him as he kneels so that his body falls on those of his kinsmen.

The Campbells march out of Glencoe driving before them two hundred horses, nine hundred cattle, and many sheep and goats....

As long as the hills stand men will remember Glencoe.

From *In Search of Scotland* by H. V. Morton

Donald Dinnie

The greatest "heavyweight" of them all?

Few sportsmen have managed to equal Donald Dinnie's record for showmanship. Cassius Clay-Muhammid Ali is a close contender. But long before Clay was using his favourite catch phrase to shock and delight the public, Dinnie was declaring "I am the greatest".

Dinnie was fortunate to be born into the Victorian era when strong men were a popular phenomenon in fairgrounds and circuses around the world. For apart from his obvious talents as an athlete he had also a natural flair for entertaining.

The handsome, kilted Scotsman performing at the Highland Games or weight-lifting on stage was very popular with women in the audience and filled men with secret admiration and envy. People flocked to see him and during his life he won more than 11 000 prizes and around £26 000 in prize money.

Dinnie rose quickly to the top of his career and has since been proclaimed Scotland's greatest athlete. He also won countless cups, shields, championship belts and medals. In keeping with his indulgence in exhibitionism, he wore his medals like a waistcoat of armour whenever he posed for photographers.

He was born on July 8, 1937 at Balnacraig, near Aboyne in Aberdeenshire. His father, Robert Dinnie, was a stone mason and poet, having several bridges, public buildings and a volume of poetry to his name.

Donald was an exceptionally bright pupil at school and especially good at languages. He left school at fifteen and became his father's apprentice in the stone mason's yard. And it wasn't long before he was issuing a challenge that he could "dress and build granite against any stone mason in the world".

He had an irresistible combination of brains and brawn together with a strong dose of ambition and a desire to win. When all these energies were released he was like a human dynamo. His complete self-confidence may have annoyed his contemporaries, but was to prove a safeguard against promoters and publicity seekers in his travels around the world.

The list of Dinnie's sporting achievements is endless. He was capable of entering and winning several events at one games meeting including putting the shot, tossing the caber, weight-throwing, jumping, hurdle racing, wrestling, dancing, pole vaulting and weight-lifting.

At sixteen he answered a challenge from the champion

heavyweight wrestler of Deeside, David Forbes. Dinnie, the young powerhouse of strength and agility, won five falls against Forbes and carried off the grand prize of £1.

His win against the reigning Deeside champion was the start of a successful athletic career which took him to all the leading Highland Games. And in his day the games were a very serious affair with high betting stakes.

But Donald Dinnie was thirty before he gave up his Stone mason's trade to become a professional athlete. By then he was already the champion of Scotland having beaten the reigning champion, William Tait of Lanarkshire, in personal contest.

Sometimes members of the audience scoffed at Dinnie's claims of strength. During one sports meeting he actually told the crowd to move back because the hammer would fall way beyond his competitors' and land in their midst. When they refused to move he threw the hammer and it soared over their heads — only then did they believe him and scatter for safety.

In 1870 Dinnie took his "all Scotch" circus to America on a triumphant tour. He was so successful that he returned for a second tour in 1877. On these tours his showmanship had mass appeal.

When he arrived to give a show in a new town, he would strut down the main street, kilt swaying and medals gleaming telling people he was the strongest, most talented, most handsome athlete in the world.

For his performances promoters paid handsomely. He could win anything between £25 and £100 if he appeared in their version of the Scottish Highland Games. But he was also quick to avoid exploitation and soon amassed a small fortune.

Dinnie had a remarkable athletic record. He beat all the champion wrestlers of Canada, Australia, New Zealand and South Africa. He also conquered the great "Muldoon", champion wrestler of America. On that famous day he won the fantastic sum — for that era — of £320.

Throughout his professional career he was beaten only on one or two occasions, once by James Fleming of Ballinluig in 1867.

Dinnie, determined to win in the end, signed Fleming to tour the world with him and proceeded to win every succeeding bout.

They returned to England via Cape Town in 1898. As a result of making a small fortune touring the world, Dinnie was able to set up business as a hotelier. During his life he owned hotels at Stonehaven, Auchinblae, Kincardine O'Neil and Brechin in Scotland in addition to similar ventures in Australia and New Zealand.

Although it would be unfair to try and compare Dinnie's athletic record with present-day standards, he still holds the record for carrying the "Dinnie Steens" at the Bridge of Potarch.

Whilst his father was repairing the bridge which crosses the River Dee near Kincardine O'Neil, he used two huge stone weights for anchors at either side of a wooden platform. Together these two stones weighed some 780 lb.

Donald, who was helping his father, picked up both stones and carried them the width of the bridge, a distance of five yards. Men have tried to stagger in his footsteps with the Dinnie stones ever since, without success. The stones now lie outside the inn at the Bridge of Potarch; travellers on horseback used to tether their horses to the rings attached to each boulder.

His name passed into legend during the First World War when the allies built a 60 lb mortar shell which the troops soon christened a "Donald Dinnie"

Each year at the Aboyne Games the Dinnie Stone Trophy is presented to the best shot putter. The holder of this trophy can look back along the tradition of Scottish athletes to the man who first used the 16 lb stone in 1867 — the father of them all, Donald Dinnie.

Jenny Outhwaite

Ian Isaac (Heavyweight Champion of Echt Show 1981) needs every kilo of his 108 kg weight to make a clear lift of the 'Dinnie Steens' which weigh over three times as much as he does.

Crowdieknowe

Oh to be at Crowdieknowe
When the last trump blaws,
An' see the deid come loupin' owre
The auld grey wa's.

Muckle men wi' tousled beards
I grat at as a bairn
'll scramble frae the croodit clay
Wi' feck o'swearin'.

An' glower at God an' a' his gang
O' angels i' the lift
—Thae trashy bleezin' French-like folk
Wha gar'd them shift!

Fain the weemun-folk'll seek
To mak' them haud their row
—*Feg, God's no blate gin he stirs up*
The men o' Crowdieknowe!

Hugh MacDiarmid

The Seven Taps of Bennachie

It is fitting that Bennachie has seven taps, for seven has the additional merit of being the number of perfection. These are: Black Hill, 1412 feet, looking away over the Brindy and the Gadie to Tap O'Noth; Craigshannoch at the north-west corner, over 1450 feet; an unnamed summit near the Mither Tap; Watch Craig, 1619 feet, with its prospect over the Don; and the two main peaks.

Of these the Mither Tap, though it is at 1698 feet the lower, is both the most difficult and the most striking. Oxen Craig, 1733 feet, the summit of which is like the head of a nowt-beast whose back throws its huge bulk right across the whole Bennachie area to the slopes above the Glenton, has no great attraction. It looks well from the Garioch as part of the whole tumbled group of tops, and on a sunny day from the Mither Tap it seems to beckon across the moorland plateau that lies between the two summits. But that is all.

It is the Mither Tap that is Bennachie. "Yon's the hill rugs at the hert when you're awa." It can rug at the hert in a different way when you are on it, as I learned one spring day. For, commencing with Craigshannoch and working widdershins (which may explain my woes), I did all the taps, ending with the Mither Tap. But it was the long haul from Turf Hill round the foot of Watch Craig and the rump of Oxon Craig to Bruntwood Tap that made me feel my muscles.

With its long heather, its carpet of deep lovely mosses, its numerous hags, and its casual water, Bennachie is not an easy hill to walk over. The Tap O'Noth, nothing like so interesting to climb or to be on, is a paradise to the feet with its firm surface and short crisp heather.

From Turf Hill to Bruntwood Tap is three miles of hard plugging and high stepping. By the time I reached the foot of the rocks on the Mither Tap I must have walked a dozen difficult miles without a pause on a breakfast of porridge and a "buttery rowie."

There was a gale blowing, I was tired and cold and hungry, and it took me some effort of will to postpone my lunch until I reached the summit. I didn't stay more than a few seconds there. If I hadn't walked off I should have been blown off.

The long road home threatened to be depressing when rain came on, but there's aye a something. When the shower was at its heaviest, I met a man on a bicycle. "Ay," he remarked, "it's lookin' a bittie like a shoo'erie." What real rain is like in the Burnhervie area I cannot imagine, never having been in the tropics.

It was a good day, not only for the physical exertion and the joy of seeing the glorious display of mosses for which Bennachie deserves to be famous. The cushions were in a score of shades, from a fresh pale green through primrose yellow to old rose, scarlet, crimson and maroon. Lovely and restful to the eyes, but singularly taxing to the locomotive muscles are the mosses of Bennachie.

I raised during the day less than a dozen grouse. It was grey weather and inclement for butterflies. In nearly five hours not a human being did I see. This was indeed the perfection of peace.

From *The Book of Bennachie* by Dr Alexander Keith

Shy Geordie

Up the Noran Water
In by Inglismaddy,
Annie's got a bairnie
That hasna got a daddy.
Some say it's Tammas's
An' some say it's Chay's;
An' naebody expec'it it,
Wi' Annie's quiet ways.

Up the Noran Water
The bonnie little mannie
Is dandled an' cuddled close
By Inglismaddy's Annie.
Wha the bairnie's daddy is
The lassie never says;
But some think it's Tammas's,
An' some think it's Chay's.

Up the Noran Water
The country folk are kind:
An' wha the bairnie's daddy is
They dinna muckle mind.
But oh! the bairn at Annie's breist,
The love in Annie's e'e —
They mak' me wish wi' a' my micht
The lucky lad was me!

Helen B. Cruickshank

Fa's Feel Are Ye?

Jamie Fleeman, the Laird of Udny's Fool, the most illustrious, was probably the very last of his order in Scotland. A real "natural" Jamie had, nevertheless, rare "glimmerings of commonsense", and possessed a pungency of ready wit and humour and a withering sarcasm which caused him to be dreaded as a foe and trusted as a friend.

A native of Longside in Aberdeenshire, Jamie was born on the 7th April 1713. He spent the days of his boyhood about the house of Sir Alexander Guthrie of Ludquharn, and at a very early period of life, began, by his bluntness of manner and shrewdness of remark, to attract the notice of his superiors. By and by he gravitated to Udny, which remained his "headquarters" during many pleasant years. He had a strange appearance. "His countenance indescribably, and even painfully, striking — wore that expression which at once betrays the absence of sound judgement; his head large and round — his hair perhaps naturally brown, but rendered, by constant exposure to the weather, of a dingy fox-colour, and not sleek, but standing on end — as if Jamie had been frightened out of his wits — indicated that his foolishness was not assumed but real". A person of strong and real affection, Jamie had equally strong and confirmed prejudices. The latter had respect to places, persons, and animals. No red-haired woman, for example, could gain his respect. "Whaur saw ye ever a lady wi' scarlet hair?" he would growl. He had a prejudice in favour of dogs, and a hatred of cats, and this, he said, was "gentlemanny". All the curs in the countryside knew him, and were glad to see him. Wherever he stayed the dog was generally permitted to share his bed and board.

Fleeman's wit was sometimes of a playful cast, sometimes of a grave nature; but grave or gay, it rarely failed to effect the object for which it was called forth. Passing along the road one day, he was accosted by a foppishly-dressed individual, who eyed him from head to foot, and exclaimed in a rather impertinent manner

"You are Udny's fool, are you not?"

"Ay," replied Jamie, with an odd stare, peculiar to himself,

"I'm Udny's feel. Fa's feel are ye?"

To an accident which befell Jamie when following his occupation as a cow-herd, is to be attributed the origin of a well known proverb widely used in the Buchan area — "The truth aye tells best." Fleeman had, in repelling the invasion of a corn-field by the cattle under his charge, resorted to the unherd-like expedient of throwing stones at the animals. One of his missiles unfortunately broke the leg of an otherwise thriving two-year-old. Towards sunset, when the hour of driving the cattle home had arrived, Jamie was lingering by a dykeside, planning an excuse for the fractured limb of the unfortunate stot. "I'll say," he soliloquised, "that he was loupin' a stank an' fell an' broke his leg. Na! that winna tell! I'll say that the brown stallion gied him a kick and did it. That winna tell either! I'll say that the park yett fell upon't. Na! that winna tell! I'll say — I'll say — what will I say? Od, I'll say that I flung a stane and did it! That'll tell!" "Ay, Jamie," cried the Laird, who had been an unseen listener, "ay, ay, Jamie, the truth aye tells best."

In the course of time Jamie was waited on to pay the debt of nature, and, while standing round his death-bed, one said to another,

"I wonder if he has any sense of another world or a future reckoning?"

"Oh, no, he is only a fool!" replied the other. "What can he know of such things?"

Jamie opened his eyes, and looking this man in the face, said, "I never heard that God seeks where he did not give."

After this he lay quiet for a short time, when he again opened his eyes, and looking up into the face of one standing near, whom he respected, he said, in a firm tone, "I'm of the gentle persuasion, dinna bury me like a beast!" And then, peacefully in that year of 1773 Jamie Fleeman quietly passed away.

His remains lie in the churchyard of Longside, in close proximity to the grave of the Rev. John Skinner, the author of "Tullochgorum"; and in kindly recognition of the humanity in poor Jamie, a handsome polished granite obelisk has been erected as near as is known to his grave, which bears the following inscription:-

Erected
In 1861
to indicate the grave
of
Jamie Fleeman
in answer to his prayer
"Dinna Bury Me Like a Beast"

From *Thistledown*
by Robert Ford

The Silver City

Yonder she sits beside the tranquil Dee,
Kindly yet cold, respectable and wise,
Sharp-tongued though civil, with wide-open eyes,
Dreaming of hills, yet urgent for the sea;
And still and on, she has her vanity,
Wears her grey mantle with a certain grace,
While sometimes there are roses on her face
To sweeten too austere simplicity.

She never taught her children fairy lore,
Yet they must go a-seeking crocks of gold
Afar throughout the earth;
And when their treasure in her lap they pour;
Her hands upon her knee do primly fold;
She smiles complacent that she gave them birth.

Marion Angus

Ibrox

The players trotted to their positions. For a moment there was dead silence over Ibrox Park. Then the whistle blew . . . .

For nearly two hours thereafter Danny Shields lived far beyond himself in a whirling world of passion. All sorts of racial emotions were released by this clash of athletic young men; the old clans of Scotland lived again their ancient hatreds in the struggle for goals. Not a man on the terraces paused to reflect that it was a spectacle cunningly arranged to draw their shillings, or to remember that the twenty-two players were so many slaves of a commercial system, liable to be bought and sold without any regard for their feelings as men. Rangers had drawn their warriors from all corners of Scotland, lads from mining villages, boys from Ayrshire farms, and even an undergraduate from the University of Glasgow. Celtic likewise had ranged the industrial belt and even crossed to Ulster and the Free State for men fit to win matches so that dividends might accrue. But for such as Danny they remained peerless and fearless warriors, saints of the Blue or the Green as it might be; and in delight in the cunning moves of them, in their tricks and ploys, the men on the terraces found release from the drabness of their own industrial hopelessness.

That release they expressed in ways extremely violent. They encouraged their favourites to dreadful deeds of assault and battery. They loudly questioned every decision of the referee. In moments of high tension they raved obscenely, using a language ugly and violent in its wealth of explosive consonants — f's and k's and b's expressing the strength of their passions.

Yet that passionate horde had its wild and joyful humours. Now and again a flash of rough jocularity would release a gust of laughter, so hearty it was as if they rejoiced to escape from the prison of their own narrow mindedness. Once in a while a clever movement by one of the opposition team would draw a mutter of unwilling but sincere admiration. They were abundantly capable of calling upon their favourites to use their brawn, but they were very strict in the observation of the unwritten laws that are called those of sportsmanship. They were, in fact, a stern but reliable jury, demanding of their entertainers the very best they could give, insisting that the spectacle be staged with all the vigour that could be brought to it.

The Old Firm — thus the evening papers described the meeting of Rangers and Celtic.

Adapted from *The Shipbuilders* by George Blake

Glasgow Street

Out of this ugliness may come,
Some day, so beautiful a flower,
That men will wonder at that hour,
Remembering smoke and flowerless slum,
And ask — glimpsing the agony
Of the slaves who wrestle to be free —
'But why were all the poets dumb?'
William Montgomerie

Whatever happened to the Lia Fail

Such were the dramatic headlines which filled the British Press on 26 December 1950; and the cause of all the consternation — the removal from Westminster of a four hundredweight block of red sandstone, variously named as: the Lia Fail or Stone of Destiny, Stone of Scone or Coronation Stone. And the perpetrators of this highly unusual and audacious deed — four young Scots: Ian Hamilton, Kay Matheson, Alan Stuart and Gavin Vernon.

In its wrath the British Establishment proclaimed the deed as: 'an act of sacrilege', 'a senseless crime' and 'mean and atrocious'. Notwithstanding, there existed a considerable and influential volume of support for the return of the 'stolen?' stone to its rightful home in Scotland. Such support included the Duke of Montrose, the Earl of Mansfield and other notable and prominent Scots.

The Stone of Destiny, itself, was that on which Scotland's kings had for generations been crowned. A powerful symbol of nationhood, it was thought that this stone had great powers and that it had been given to an early Celtic king who married the daughter of an Egyptian Pharaoh. The Princess was named Scota, from whom the Scots are supposed to have adopted their name — so says the legend. The Stone was seized by Edward I the 'Hammer of the Scots', after he conquered Scotland in 1296, and to symbolize that Scotland was no longer to remain a kingdom, he ordered the removal of the 'Stone' to Westminster Abbey. When the Scots regained their independence under Robert the Bruce, the return of the 'Stone' was a condition of the peace made with England. The restoration of the 'Stone', however, was never accomplished, as after agreeing to do so in the Treaty of Northampton, the English broke their word and the 'Stone' remained in the Coronation Chair in Westminster Abbey — a fact conveniently overlooked by the establishment ever since!

In his highly entertaining book, *No Stone Unturned*, the ringlead-

57

er of the 1950 exploit provides a gripping account of the events which led to the recapture of the 'Stone' by the four young Scots. All sorts of unexpected things happened during the exploit, including the following incident: while the stone is actually being removed from the Coronation Chair by two of the men, a policeman approaches the getaway car outside the Abbey in which the other two are waiting.

The policeman loomed up in front of us. "What's going on here?" he thundered. It was perfectly obvious what was going on. Kay and I did not fall apart until he had had plenty of opportunity to see us.

"It's Christmas Eve, you know, officer," I explained.

"Christmas Eve be damned!" he answered. "It's five o'clock on Christmas morning."

"Ochone! Ochone!" I said. "Is it that time already?"

"You're sitting on private property here," he told us. "And why did you move forward when you saw me coming?"

"I know," I said humbly. "I knew we shouldn't be here. We put on the lights to show you that we were quite willing to move on."

"But where can we go?" asked Kay, vamping him. "The streets are far too busy."

"You should be off home," he told her, and looked at her severely.

We explained to him that we were down from Scotland on tour, and that we had arrived in London too late to get a bed. We sat and held hands in front of him, and tried to give him the impression that we were too much in love to go to a hotel and be parted.

He began to warm to us. To my horror, he took off his helmet, and laid it on the roof of the car. He lit a cigarette and showed every sign of staying till he had smoked it.

"There's a dark car park just along the road," he said, smacking his lips contemplatively. We knew that car park. The other car was there.

"Och, well," said Kay, thrusting her head into the lion's mouth, "if we're not comfortable there we can always get you to run us in and give us a bed in the cells."

"No! No!" said the P.C. knowingly. "There's not a policeman in London would arrest you tonight. None of them want to appear in Court on Boxing Day to give evidence against you." Kay gave my hand a squeeze.

"A good night for crime!" I said, and we all laughed . . . .

All this time I had been conscious of a scraping going on behind the hoarding. Why on earth didn't they lie low until the policeman had gone? It transpired afterwards that they had no idea that we were entertaining the police, and they were calling my parentage in question to the tenth generation for sitting in the car while they did all the work.

Kay heard the noise too, and we engaged the constable in furious conversation. He thought us excellent company. His slightest sally brought forth peals of laughter, and when he essayed a joke we nearly had convulsions. Surely they would hear our laughter and be warned.

There was a muffled thud from behind the hoarding. The constable stopped speaking, tensed, listened. My heart sank to my boots. Kay's hand became rigid in mine. Then the constable laughed and said. "That was the old watchman falling down the stairs." Furiously and hysterically, Kay and I laughed at the idea of the watchman falling down the stairs. Surely they had heard us now.

"I wish it was six o'clock," said the policeman. "And then I would be off duty."

Out of the corner of my eye, I saw the door in the hoarding slowly opening. Gavin's face appeared, followed by his hand and shoulders. Suddenly he froze. He had seen the policeman. His lips formed an amazed oath. Inch by inch he edged back, and the door closed behind him. The policeman finished his cigarette and put on his helmet. "You'd better be going now," he said.

"We had indeed!" I said, wiping the sweat out of my eyes.

"Will you show us the way?" asked Kay, trying to get him off the premises.

"Oh, you can't miss the park," he said, and redirected us.

Kay started the engine. She is, although she will be annoyed that I say so, a very bad driver, but that morning her bad driving was by design and not incompetence. Never has clutch been let in so jerkily; never has a car veered from side to side so crazily. I looked back and waved to the constable. As Kay had expected he was following down behind us — too amazed at the crazy driving to pay attention to anything else.

After collecting the 'Stone' and the other two accomplices, they eventually brought it back to Scotland and gave it into the care of the Church of Scotland. It was placed in Arbroath Abbey.

We did not know what was going to happen, but it could not then have stopped us. We arranged to have the Stone repaired by the best mason in Scotland. We drafted a petition to the King, reaffirming our loyalty and repeating our claim for just government, and finally we prepared a letter to the Church of Scotland, to whom we decided to hand the Stone as the successors of the Abbots of Scone, from whom the Stone had been originally stolen.

We chose as the place to expose the Stone the ruined Abbey of Arbroath where in 1320 the Estates of Scotland had met to reaffirm their freedom with the sound of the North Sea in their ears and the smell of their burnt homes still in their nostrils.

On the morning of April 11th 1951, I left Glasgow with Neil. At Stirling Bridge we thumbed a car which was driven by Councillor Gray and which contained the Stone of Destiny. At midday we carried the Stone down the grass-floored nave of Arbroath Abbey and left it at the high altar. It was a crucifixion.

When we turned away and stood for a minute at the gate and looked down the long nave flanked by the blood-red sandstone of the walls to the altar where the Stone lay under a saltire, I heard the voice of Scotland speak as clearly as it spoke in 1320:

> For so long as a hundred of us are left alive we will yield in no least way to English domination. We fight not for glory nor wealth nor for honour, but only and alone for freedom, which no good man surrenders but with his life.

I never saw the Stone again.

From *No Stone Unturned* by Ian Hamilton

The authorities chose to hustle the Stone back over the border to Westminster once more. But did they get the 'real' Stone?

The Famous Tay Whale

Literary composition is an art, and, like other arts, is governed by certain rules and limitations — we might even say conventions. In rhymed verse a certain amount of harmony is usually considered necessary. It is one of the elements totally lacking in the writings of William McGonagall. Rhythm and measure, also, have been considered from time immemorial as essential to the making of good verse, but rhythm and measure were cast aside when this bard took up his pen.

Throughout his life, McGonagall held a belief in the strength and power of his literary art, which seems to have been absolute. Often the butt of cruel and heartless jokes and jibes at the hands of his contemporaries, educated and otherwise, McGonagall has, nevertheless, had the last laugh — for it is he whom history remembers with a kindly smile, not his tormentors. McGonagall, who immortalized so many aspects and events of life around him, has, in his own way, by his own style, been himself immortalized. Perhaps the key to the life and writings of the enigmatic McGonagall may lie in the adapted tenet of the philosophy of Virgil, namely:

> He could, because
> he thought he could.

Much of the poet's literary output concerned the life and times of the city of his adopted residence — Dundee. In the following poem, McGonagall in his inimitable style, writes for posterity the saga of:

The Famous Tay Whale

'Twas in the month of December, and in the year of 1883,
That a monster whale came to Dundee,
Resolved for a few days to sport and play,
And devour the small fishes in the silvery Tay.

So the monster whale did sport and play
Among the innocent little fishes in the beautiful Tay,
Until he was seen by some men one day,
And they resolved to catch him without delay.

When it came to be known a whale was seen in the Tay
Some men began to talk and to say —
"We must try and catch this monster of a whale,
So come on, brave boys, and never say fail."

Then the people together in crowds did run,
Resolved to capture the whale and to have some fun;
So small boats were launched on the silvery Tay,
While the monster of the deep did sport and play.

Oh! it was a most fearful and beautiful sight,
To see it lashing the water with its tail all its might,
And making the water ascend like a shower of hail,
With one lash of its ugly and mighty tail.

Then the water did descend on the men in the boats,
Which wet their trousers and also their coats;
But it only made them the more determined to catch the whale,
But the whale he shook at them his tail.

Then the whale began to puff and blow,
Then the men and boats after him did go,
Armed well with harpoons for the fray,
Which they fired at him without dismay.

And they laughed and grinned just like wild baboons,
While they fired at him their sharp harpoons:
But when struck with the harpoons he dived below,
Which filled his pursuers' hearts with woe.

Because they guessed that they had lost a prize,
Which caused the tears to well up in their eyes;
And in that their anticipations were only right,
Because he sped on to Stonehaven with all his might.

And was first seen by the crew of a Gourdon fishing boat,
Which they thought was a big coble upturned afloat;
But when they drew near they saw it was a whale,
So they resolved to tow it ashore without fail.

So they got a rope from each boat tied round his tail,
And landed their burden at Stonehaven without fail;
And when the people saw it their voices they did raise,
Declaring that the brave fishermen deserved great praise.

And my opinion is that God sent the whale in time of need,
No matter what other people may think or what is their creed;
I know fishermen in general are often very poor
And God in his goodness sent it to drive poverty from their door.

So John Wood has bought it for two hundred and twenty-six
    pounds,
And has brought it to Dundee all safe and all sound;
Which measures 40 feet in length from the snout to the tail,
So I advise the people far and near to see it without fail.

Then hurrah for the mighty monster whale!
Which has got 17 feet 4 inches, from tip to tip, of a tail;
Which can be seen for a sixpence or a shilling,
That is to say if the people all are willing.

William McGonagall

Last Lauch

The Minister said it wad dee,
the cypress bush I plantit.
But the bush grew til a tree,
naething dauntit.

Hit's growin, stark and heich,
derk and straucht and sinister,
kirkyairdie-like and dreich.
But whaur's the Minister?

Douglas Young

Rach-ma-Reeshil

Rach-ma-reeshil could be defined as a mixture of proverbs, sayings, epitaphs, superstitions and the like — 'a' throuther.'

THE WIRD

A B brod n: A board with the letters of the alphabet painted on it for use by school children.

> They gied me first the A B brod,
> Whilk ser't for shool, for book and rod.

Beistie-milk, n: The first milk of a cow after calving, which when boiled takes on a consistency like new-made cheese.
Brose, n: An oatmeal dish on which boiling water is poured and then stirred in until the water and meal are thoroughly mixed.

> Sowens is watery meat,
>   And kail a blash o' brue;
> Parritch is meat for a man,
>   And brose is 'clag'm too.

Chuckie-stanes, n: Small stones, fragments of quartz, as found in the crops of chuckies or hens.

> Your stamack wad grun chuckie-stanes.
> > *Old proverb*

Dead-kist, n: A coffin.

Farl, n: A quarter segment of oat cake.

Gled, n: The kite, buzzard.
An old saying "Fa'un frae the gled", describes a dishevelled person, as if rescued from the claws of a bird of prey.

64

Hurl-come-gush, n: A great and sudden rush, used to describe the mountain burns after a heavy thunder-plout. Also used to describe a torrent of words.

Jaup, v: Used of liquid contents of a vessel, to splash.

> Auld Scotland wants nae skinking ware
> That jaups in luggies;
> But if ye want her gratefu' prayer,
> Gie her a Haggis!

Lair, lear, lere, n: Learning, knowledge.

> I wadna be an orra loon
> For a' the warld's gear!
> O, I widna be an orra loon,
> I'd raither stick te lear!

Lowping-on-stane, n: A set of stone steps used by women and the infirm to mount a horse.

Maukin, n: A hare.
An old superstition suggests that it brings ill luck to see a maukin cross the road in the early morning.

Moullie-heils, n: Chilblains.
A superstitious cure for this ailment recommends the sufferer to visit a strange door at dark of night, and tap gently. When asked "Wha's there?" Make the immediate reply, "Moullie-heils, Tak ye them there," and so transfer the complaint to the person inside.

Neivie-nick-nack, n: A guessing-game played with the 'neives' fists.

> Neivie, neivie, nick-nack,
> Which han' will ye tak?
> Tak the richt, tak the wrang,
> I'll beguile ye if I can.
>   Children's rhyme

Palmy, n: A blow on the palm of the hand from a schoolmaster's 'tawse'.

Queinzie, n: A corner.

> O where are all my merry men,
>   I land paid meat and fee,
> Who will pull out the queinzie stane
>   And let the flame go free.

Rottan, n: A rat.

The following superstitious rhyme was often written on the walls of 'rottan' infested houses as a charm.

> Rottan and moose,
> Lea' the puir woman's hoose;
> Gang owre tae the mill,
> And there ane and a' ye'll get yer fill.

Shirramuir, n: A confused and tumultous quarrel; from the battle of Sherrifmuir (1715) between rebels and King's troops. Used to described a quarrel as:

> "Sic a Shirra-muir," such a quarrel.

Stepmither's Scone, n: Used to describe the often meagre allowance of the stepmother to her poor wards; as from the thin skin of common scones (made from barley meal and raised up by heat and having no substance).

Yill, n: Beer, ale.

> And though you may me kill,
> I'll not you tell
> How we brew yill
> From the heather bell.

COUNTING OUT RHYMES

Eettle, ottle, black bottle
Eettle, ottle, oot
If you want a piece on jam
Just call oot

Zeenty, teenty, fickety, faig,
Zell, dell, domin, aig,
Zirky, birky, starry, rock,
Am, tan, toosht.

(19th century)

Eesy, osy,
Mannie's nosie
Eesy, osy
Out

(19th century)

Eenertee, feenertee, fichertie, fag,
Ell, dell, dolman's egg.
Irkie, birkie, starry rock,
Ann, tam, toosh, Jock.
Black puddin', white troot,
That shows you're oot.

Eenty, teenty, tippenny bun,
The cat geed oot to get some fun;
She got some fun, she played drum
Eenty, teenty, tippenny bun.

(19th century)

Hoky, poky, penny pie
Stan' ye oot by.

(19th century)

CHILDREN'S GAMES

One stands in middle. The rest walk round in a ring singing:

Green grosets, green grosets, the grass is so green
The hansomest fellow that ever was seen.
We washed him, we dried him, and clothed him in silk
And we wrote down his name with a gold pen and ink.
O Annie O Annie; your true love is dead
And we send you a letter to turn round your head.

The chosen one turns and faces outwards.
This is repeated until all are turned facing outwards.

A ring is formed. Sally kneels in the middle covering her face (crying).

Sally, Sally, Water   (*The ring dancing round*)
Sprinkle in the pan
Rise, Sally; Rise, Sally   (*Sally stands*)
Choose a young man.

Bow to the east   (*Sally bows*)
And bow to the west   (*Sally bows*)
And bow to the one   (*Sally bows*)
That you love best.   (*Sally chooses*)

And now you're married, we wish you joy
First a girl and then a boy
Seven years after, son and daughter
Clasping hands; come out of the water.   (*The chosen then takes Sally's place.*)

BALL GAMES

When I was one
I went to school
To learn my A.B.C.
So I jumped aboard the Captain's ship
And the Captain said to me
Oh this way
And that way
Forward and backway
And thats your A.B.C.

Are you going to golf, sir?
No sir, why sir?
Because I've got a cold, sir
Where did you catch a cold, sir?
At the North Pole, sir
What were you doing there, sir?
Catching polar bears, sir
How many did you catch, sir?
One sir, two sir
Three sir, four sir
And many many more sir

Matthew, Mark, Luke and John
Next door neighbour carry on

You need two to play this and two balls. The first one says the rhyme then the other one catches the balls and carries on.

Mrs Dunlop had a wee shop
And all she sold was candy rock
Candy rock, a penny a stick
Take a lick and let one drop

You do ordinary doublers until you come to the last line. You put your hand up to your mouth then catch the ball and make the other ball drop once.

Away up in Holland,
The land of the Dutch;
There lives a wee lassie
I love very much;
Her name is Susanna,
But where is she now?
She's down in the meadow
A milking a cow.

Up the river
Down the sea
Tommy broke a window
Blamed it on me;
I told my Ma
She told my Pa,
Tommy got a leathering,
Ha! Ha! Ha!

1, 2, 3, a lady,
4, 5, 6, a lady,
7, 8, 9, a lady,
10 a lady postman.

SKIPPING GAMES

All in Together Girls

All, all, all in together girls
Never mind the weather
When I say your birthday
Leave the ropes empty

January, February, March, April, May,
June, July, August, September, October,
November, December.

When it is your birthday, you jump out of the rope.

Solomon Grundy

Solomon Grundy
Born on Monday
Christened on Tuesday
Married on Wednesday
Ill on Thursday
Worse on Friday
Died on Saturday
Buried on Sunday
And that was the end of Solomon Grundy

Rock the rope gently from side to side. While one person jumps over it, the two people at the ends say the rhyme.

Kings and Queens

Kings and Queens and jelly beans please jump in
Kings and Queens and jelly beans please pass over
Kings and Queens please jump out.

When it says 'please jump in', jump in. when it says 'pass over', pass over with your partner. When it says 'please jump out', jump out.

Circus Strong-Man

"Circus strong-man sad to say
Looked in the mirror
And passed away"

This is a skipping game in which each person tries to do one jump in turn without missing a rope. To miss a rope is to leave the rope with no one jumping in it. Circus strong-man is easy once you get the hang of it.

Blue bells
coral shells
eevie eevie over
here comes the teacher
with the big fat stick
now get ready
for your arithmetic
two plus two is four
now get ready
for your spelling
C.A.T. spells cat
D.O.G. spells dog
now get ready
for your hot dogs.

Standing at the bar
Smoking a cigar
Woompilala, Woompilala
Standing at the bar

Jump for the first line, pretend your're smoking in the second line, put your arms and legs
out to the sides in the third line, and jump
again for the last line.

On a mountain
Stands a castle,
Who's the owner?
Frankenstein!
And his daughter
Pansy Potter
'She my only Valentine.
So I call in (...) dear, (...) dear,
So I call in (...) dear,
And I'll go out till next New Year.

I have a little bubble-car, number 48,
Drove it round the corner and jammed on the brake.

Vote, Vote, Vote for (Harold Wilson)
In comes Margaret at the door,
Margaret is the one
We all like the best
So we don't want Harold any more —
Shut the door!

Not last night but the night before
Twenty-five robbers came to my door,
As I went out they said to me,
"Spanish lady, turn around,
Spanish lady, touch the ground,
Spanish lady do high kicks,
Spanish lady do the splits."

Cowboy Joe from Mexico,
Hands up, stick 'em up,
Don't forget to pick 'em up,
Cowboy Joe.

1,2,3, high, low, slow,
medium, dolly, rocky,
hoppy, skippy, jumpy,
pepper, salt.
(Rope held according to word.)

Have you Ever Ever

Have you ever, ever, ever in your long legged life
Seen a long legged sailor
With a long legged wife
No I never, never, never in my long legged life
Saw a long legged sailor
With a long legged wife

This is a rhyme for elastics (Chinese skipping). Do splits going
from one side to another all the time, except when you say *long*,
put your legs over the elastics.

BELIEFS

The man in the moon was put there for cutting sticks (fire-
wood) on Sunday.
If you look between a horse's ears at night you can see evil.
It's unlucky to comb your hair at night time — a friend or
relation might fall or have an accident.
It's unlucky to give away salt.
It's unlucky to take a burning stick from a campfire — to
carry off the flame is to carry off luck.
Throw a piece of steel or iron (a nail) in a burn when crossing
it at night; then no evil spirits can cross after you.
Put a needle in baby's bonnet for protection against witches
or fairies.
It's unlucky to see the back end of the first spring lamb or
foal; but it's lucky to see its face.
The devil let his imps go on Hallowe'en night to spit on the
brambles: anyone eating brambles after Hallowe'en is taken
over by evil spirits.
It's unlucky to burn holly or to cut it. If you want a piece,
break it; for Jesus Christ was crowned with a crown of holly
— the berries are red from His blood.
Animals know more about religion than any person:

On Christmas Eve no animal will eat between twelve midnight and one o'clock: the donkey, the cow and the horse — even though they are hungry — will stop eating for this hour on Christmas Eve. Any other night they may eat (or chew their cuds) the whole night through.

The donkey goes down on its knees at twelve o'clock on Christmas Eve, from twelve to one.

No person will ever see a donkey dying. You can sit with it, although it's seriously ill, for hours and it will still have a breath in its body. Suppose you turn your back on it for a minute — it will be gone. But you will never watch it dying. For it was the donkey that carried Baby Jesus to Bethlehem; this was its gift — no one will ever see it dying.

Why the robin's breast is red.

If you sit in the middle of the forest, the only bird that will come up to you is the robin. It doesn't matter where you stop — a robin will come up to you. They say the same thing happened at the Crucifixion. He's a curious bird, the robin. When he walked up to the Crucifixion a drop of blood fell on his chest from the Crucifixion.

If you bake a scone on Good Friday and throw a piece of it to a hungry raven, he won't eat it; even though he might be dying of hunger, he'll not touch it, not even the next day — he'll know it's been made on Good Friday. If you take a piece of bread baked on the day before, Thursday, he will eat it. But you can't deceive it. Because the raven came back with a leaf to Noah — Noah let the raven out of the ark first because the raven was strong and could fly faster and farther than other birds.

From the oral narration of
Duncan Williamson

APHORISMS

There's nae rainy days in his week! (a braggart)
He's delicate! (a fat person)
His race is all run! (a slow person)
I'll be a fit afore ye! (I'll be up in the morning before you.)
Heaven'll no' be his bed! (evil person)
Some day his foot'll miss a stile! (He's been getting away with too much.)
Every drop would fill a ladle! (heavy rain)
His boots would never go on my feet! (I wouldn't like to be in his place.)
Cut the gutter! (Clear out!)
He could beat the globe! (He was clever.)
His face was like thunder! (He was dour.)
His face was like matches! (He was robust, rosy-cheeked.)
Her skin was like milk! (She had a lovely complexion.)
His porridge was thin! (skinny man, reared on thin porridge)
The cock'll no' crow in his morning! (sleepy-headed person)
It'll be a cauld fit and a warm yin before I'm here again! (don't like the place)
His time 'll no' be richt! (He's a wee bit backward.)
Sigh it! (Stop speaking about that.)
Rough it! (Curse it [him, her, anything].)
He wouldn't sell his hen on a wet day! (a thrifty person)

From the oral narration of Duncan Williamson

RIDDLES

There was a man o' Adam's race,
He had a certain dwelling-place;
It was neither in heeven, earth, nor hell —
Tell me where this man did dwell!

(Jonah in the whale's belly)

Pease-porridge hot, pease-porridge cold,
Pease-porridge in a caup, nine days old.
Tell me that in four letters.

(T.H.A.T.)

Come a riddle, come a riddle,
Come a rot-tot-tot,
A little wee man in a bricht red coat
Wi' a stick in his hand
And a stane in his throat,
Come a riddle, come a riddle
Come a rot-tot-tot.

(A cherry)

A wee, wee hoose, fu', fu' o' meat
Wi' naither door nor winda tae lat me intae eat.

(An egg)

Wee man o' leather
Gaed through the heather
Through a rock, through a reel,
Through an auld spinning-wheel,
Through a sheep-shank bane;
Sic a man was never seen.

(A beetle)

Lang legs and nae knees
Roond feet like bawbees

(Tongs)

The flooer o' France and the fruit o'Spain
Met thegither in a shooer o' rain,
Rowed in a clout, tied wi' a string,
If ye tell me that, I'll gie ye a gowd ring.

(A dumpling)

Whit gaes intae the burn white and comes oot black?

(A baker's bool)

Riddlum, Riddleum

As I gaed ower the Brig o' Dee
I met Geordie Buchan;
I took aff his heed, and drank his bleed,
An left his body standin.

(A bottle of whisky.)

A've a wee hoose o' strae,
That A didna gaither—
It's warm an it's cool,
In aa sorts o' waither.
A've thoosands o' sisters,
But no a richt brither,
An ma feyther deid
Faun he mairied ma mither.
A wark nicht an day
Wi mickle tae shaw,
An when aa's weel won
It's aa stolen awa.
Tho A'm maist weel contentit
Ma temper is frail,
Sae haud weel ahint me,
Ma stang's in ma tail.

(A bee.)

RIDDLES
from Duncan Williamson

As I went out and in again
Out of the dead life did come —
Six there are and seven shall be —
For soon a free man I will be.

(A prisoner in jail in long-gone times was asked to make up an unanswerable riddle for his freedom. While walking out for his exercise he sees a wren's nest in an old cow's skull — there are six fledglings and one egg soon to hatch. He knows no one will ever guess the answer.)

As I came over London bridge
I met a London scholar:
I drew off his hat and drank his blood
And left his body standing.

(A bottle of beer sitting on the bridge.)

There were two riders passing by —
There were six apples hanging high
"Each" took one —
How many were left?

(Five; "Each" was one rider's name.)

76

There was a king 'at met a king
In a dry lane;
Says a king to a king,
"Where have you been?"
"I have bane in the wood,
    Bane huntin' a roe."
"Would you call your dog to you
    And tell me its name?"
"I have told you twice already,
    I won't tell you again."
What was the dog's name?

("Bane.")

A long thing nakit
Through the field streakit —
Take in your dogs
But put out your hens!

(A large worm)

John Hotton, John Totton,
He came from Barrhead —
He was buried and rotten
Before he was dead;
He was rotten before he was gotten
And gotten before he was rotten.

(A potato)

Down in the meadow there grows green and yellow —
The king couldn't read it nor yet could the lord,
They sent for three wise men out of the east —
It had hundreds of horns but wasn't a beast.
What was it?

(A whin bush)

Down in the meadow there it stands
Ten feet and two hands,
Lights and livers and lives three
What kind of animal can it be?

(A ploughman and his horses)

Upon oak leaves I stand
Under the ground I am,
I ride on a filly that never was foaled
And I carry the dead in my hand.

(A farmer was called to court in bygone times. He was offered the choice of going to jail or making up an unanswerable riddle. Many years before that his favourite mare which was in foal was dying, so he opened up her stomach and took out the foal. He made a whip from a piece of the mare's skin which he had kept. He filled his boots with oak leaves and earth; he rode on the filly to court and carried the whip in his hand.)

Two legs sat upon three legs
With four legs on his lap,
When in comes four legs
Runs away with one leg,
Up jumps two legs
Catches a hold of three legs
Flings it after four legs
And makes him bring one leg back!

(*A man cutting up a sheep is sitting on a three-legged stool; in comes a dog and runs away with one of the sheep's legs. The man jumps up, flings the stool at the dog and makes it bring back the sheep's leg.*)

Mister, mister, get up off your easy-greasy
Put on your tartan takkers,
White-faced dorby is runnin' up the bone trampers
Cock-a-lour's on his back
Your house is in danger!

(*A man is sitting half asleep on his chair by the fireside when a hot cinder from the fire falls on the cat's back and makes the cat run up the stairs — with the hot cinder on its back which might set the house on fire.*)

As I went o'er the moor of muddy
I met an auld woman who was cawin' a cuddy,
"Cuddy!" she cried and gave it a whip
And all the hair came curlin' up.

(*An old lady spinning at a spinning wheel.*)

There was an auld lady she wasnae a fool
She made White stockings out of Black sheeps' wool
And she made Black stocking out of White sheeps' wool,
She never used dye of any description —
How did the auld lady do it?

(*Mr Black kept white sheep and Mr White kept black sheep. So she borrowed wool from one to make stockings for the other!*)

From the oral narration of Duncan Williamson

THE LAST LAUCHS
— a selection of kirkyard humour

One of the strongest and most worthwhile aspects of Scottish humour is that Scots, unlike many other races, can take a good laugh at their own expense; and as one can see in the following selection of epitaphs — even in death.

From Aberdeenshire:

Here lyes William Forbes of New, who
departed this life, the 10th January, 1638.
Remember man, as thou goes by,
As thou art now, so once was I,
As I am now, so thou must be;
Remember, man, that thou must die.

From Banffshire:

Here lies interred a man o' micht
   His name was Malcolm Downie:
He lost his life ae market nicht
   By fa'in aff his pownie.
            Aged 37 years.

From Perthshire:

The tombstone of Marion Scott, who died at the age of 100 at Dunkeld, on November 21, 1727, declares:

Stop, passenger, until my life you've read;
The living may get knowledge by the dead.
Five times five years I liv'd a virgin life;
Five times five years I was a virtuous wife;
Ten times five years I liv'd a widow chaste;
Now, tir'd of this mortal life, I rest.

I, from my cradle to my grave, have seen
Eight mighty kings of Scotland, and a queen,
Full twice five years the Commonwealth I saw;
Ten times the subjects rose against the law.
Twice did I see the old prelacy pull'd down!
And twice the cloak was humbled by the gown.
An end of Stuart's race I saw: nay more!
I saw my country sold for English ore.
Such desolations in my time have been;
I have an end of all perfection seen.

Remember man
As thou goes by,
As thou art now
So once was I
As I am now
So thou must be,
Remember man
that thou must die.

Janet Milne, spouse to
James Lurie, her Monument
   We do this for no ither end
   But that our Burial may be ken'd.

       and:

Here lies the Smith-to wit-Tam Gouk
His Faither and his Mither,
Wi' Tam, and Jock, and Joan and Noll,
And a' the Gouks thegither.
When on the yird Tam and his wife
Greed desperate ill wi'ither,
But noo, without e'en fin or strife,
They tak' their Nap thegither.

From Aberdeenshire:

Whaa lies here?
John Sim, ye needna' spier.
Hullo, John, is that you?
Ay, ay, but I'm deed noo.

Written on the Eve of his Execution

Let them bestow on every airt a limb,
Then open all my veins that I may swim
To thee, my Maker, in that crimson lake;
Then place my parboiled head upon a stake,
Scatter my ashes — strew them in the air—
Lord! since thou knowest where all these atoms are,
I'm hopeful thou'lt recover once my dust,
And confident thou'lt raise me with the just.

          James Graham, Marquis of Montrose

On a gravestone in Forfar cemetery:

'Tis here that Tibbie Allan lies —
'Tis here, or here aboot.
But naebody till the Resurrection Day
Can the very spot dispute.

Hame and Schule

Hame, in pre-television days was a place of great sociability. Although often overcrowded and sparsely furnished, the social atmosphere of the 'extended' family hame of earlier times may well have been much warmer and more friendly than the cool, comfortable surroundings of the modern 'nuclear' family.

In contrast, *schule* in the past twenty-five years has developed a warmth and spontaneity sorely lacking in too many schools in the 'good old days'. Increasing numbers of pupils today actually enjoy school. This is probably due to the lessening of 'academic' pressures and the development of wider and more interesting curricula devised to suit children of all abilities and not merely for the benefit of the top ten per cent of the school population. Gone, thankfully, are the days when certain teachers would write alongside the sums on the blackboard, the dreaded abbreviation B.I.W. — Belt if wrong!

Hamewith

Hot youth ever is a ranger,
   New scenes ever its desire;
Cauld Eild, doubtfu' o' the stranger,
   Thinks but o' haudin in the fire.

Midway, the wanderer is weary,
   Fain he'd be turnin' in his prime
Hamewith-the road that's never dreary,
   Back where his heart is a' the time.

Charles Murray

The Flit

Wild weather it was that January and the night on the Slug road smoring with sleet when John Guthrie crossed his family and gear from Aberdeen into the Mearns. Twice the great carts set with their shelvins that rustled still stray binder-twine from September's harvest-home laired in drifts before the ascent of the Slug faced the reluctant horses. Darkness came down like a wet, wet blanket, weariness below it and the crying of the twins to vex John Guthrie. Mother called him from her nook in the leading cart, there where she sat with now one twin at the breast and now another, and her rust-gold hair draped down from the darkness about her face into the light of the swinging lantern: *"We'd better loosen up at Portlethen and not try the Slug this night."*

My father swore at that: *"Damn't to hell, do you think I'm made of silver to put up the night at Portlethen?"* and mother sighed and held off the wee twin, Robert, and the milk dripped creamily from the soft sweet lips of him: *"No, we're not made of silver, but maybe we'll lair again and all die of the night."*

Maybe he feared that himself, John Guthrie, his rage was his worriment with the night, but he'd no time to answer her for a great bellowing arose in the road by the winding scurry of peat-moss that lined the dying light of the moon. The cattle had bunched there, tails to the wind, refusing the Slug and the sting of the sleet, little Dod was wailing and crying at the beasts, Polled Angus and Shorthorns and half-bred Highland stirks who had fattened and feted and loved their life in the haughs of Echt, south there across the uncouthy hills was a world cold and unchancy.

But John Guthrie dropped the tarpaulin edge that shielded his wife and the twins and the furnishings of the best room and gear good and plentiful enough; and swiftly he ran past the head of the horse till he came to where the cattle bunched. And he swung Dod into the ditch with one swipe of his hand and cried, *"Have you got no sense, you brat?"* and uncoiled from his hand the length of hide that served him as a whip. Its crackle snarled down through the sting of the sleet, and the hair rose in long serrations across the back of the cattle, and one in a minute, a little Highland steer it was, mooed and ran forward and fell to a trot, and the rest

82

followed after, slipping and sprawling with their cloven hooves, the reek of their dung sharp and bitter in the sleet smore of the night. Ahead Alex saw them coming and turned himself about again, and fell to a trot, leading up the Slug to Mearns and the South.

So, creaking and creaking, and the shelvins skirling under the weight of their loads, they passed that danger point, the carts plodded into motion again, the first with its hooded light and house gear and Mother suckling the twins. In the next, Clyde's cart, the seed was loaded, potato and corn and barley, and bags of tools and implements, and graips and forks fast tied with esparto twine and two fine ploughs and a driller, and dairy things and a turnip machine with teeth that cuts as a guillotine cuts. Head down to the wind and her reins loose and her bonny coat all mottled with sleet went Clyde, the load a nothing to her, fine and clean and sonsy she marched following John Guthrie's cart with no other thing or soul to guide her but that ever and now, in this half-mile and that she heard his voice cry cheerily; *"Fine, Clyde, fine. Come on then, lass."*

Chris and Will with the last cart, sixteen Will and fifteen Chris, the road wound up and up, straight and unwavering, and sometimes they hiddled in the lithe and the sleet sang past to left and right, white and glowing in the darkness. And sometimes they clambered down from the shelvins above the laboured drag of old Bob and ran beside him, one on either side, and stamped for warmth in their feet, and saw the whin bushes climb black the white hills beside them and far and away the blink of lights across the moors where folk lay happed and warm. But then upwards the road would swerve, right or left, into this steep ledge or that, and the wind would be at them again and they'd gasp, climbing back into the shelvins, Will with freezing feet and hands and the batter of sleet like needles in his face. Chris in worse case, colder and colder at every turn, her body numb and unhappy, knees and thighs and stomach and breast, so that she nearly wept. But of that she told nothing, she fell to a drowse through the cold, and a strange dream came to her as they plodded up through the ancient hills.

For out of the night ahead of them came running a man, father didn't see him or heed to him, though old Bob in the dream that was Chris' snorted and shied. And as he came he wrung his hands, he was mad and singing, a foreign creature, black-bearded and half-naked he was; and he cried in the Greek *"The ships of Pytheas! The ships of Pytheas!"* and went by into the smore of the sleet-storm on the Grampian hills. Chris never saw him again, queer dreaming that was. For her eyes were wide open, she rubbed them with never a need of that, if she hadn't been dreaming she must have been daft. They'd cleared the Slug, below was Stonehaven and the Mearns, and far beyond that, miles through the Howe, the twinkling point of light shone from the flagstaff of Kinraddie.

So that was their coming to Blawearie, fell wearied all of them were the little of the night that was left them, and slept late into the next morning, coming cold and drizzly up from the sea by Bervie.

From *Sunset Song* by Lewis Grassic Gibbon

Short Back and Sides

"An' ye ken faur you're gaun the morn, efter the schule," mither would say pointedly. Tae get that hair o' yours cut," she would vex. "It's fair tormentin' me, hingin' owre yer collar like that. Mind noo, richt efter the schule!"

Next efterneen, wi' yer sixpence in yer han', owre ye would traik tae Sandy Barclay's Barber Shop. The auld mannies sittin' on the seat ootside, under the candy-strippit pole, would gley up an' say,

"Aye laddie, yer fair needin' a barbarazin',"

An' then snicher an' cackle tae themsels'. Naebody telt them faun tae get their hair cut!

Mind you, aince ye got intae the shop it wisna sae bad. It was an interestin' kind o' place, even tho' Sandy was there tae cut aff yer hair. There was aye ane or twa folk sittin' waitin' for a shave or a haircut, or maybe even a shampoo. It was kinda like bein' in a play, folk speakin' aboot things for the sake o' brakin' the monotony o' the steady snip, snip fae Sandy's shears; faun they'd really much raither be haen' their tea or diggin' their gairdens.

Tae ca' Sandy's shop a 'shop' was maybe a bit grand. It was really jist the front room o' his hoose, which lookit' richt oot ontae the street. It was a lang, dreich room, wi' dark green, sharny coloured distemper on the wa's. Half a dizen chairs and a lang bench were lined up against the back wa', for the assorted clients. Facin' the opposite wa' there were twa big, black widden barber's chairs, an' a stool that fittit' intae ane o' the chairs — for the wee loons. The rest o' the 'equipment' was a sink screwed intae the wa', a blotchy, stained mirror, a shelf for Sandy's clippers and shears an' the big jar o' cream tae clart on yer hair faun the 'operation' was owre. The 'piece de resistance' was Sandy's gas het-watter geyser. Sandy was fair prood o' his gas lichts an' his geyser — and bein' the only anes in the district, the customers were fell prood o' them as weel. The lichts sighed softly, hiccuped and plopped in their ain mysterious language, like some eldricht craturs fae the depths o' space.

In the far corner o' the room was a narrow, black, coffin-like door that led ben tae the rest o' the hoose. It was at that door that Sandy's missus, Nancy, would appear; usually tae get on tae Sandy aboot something, an' aye in front o' a' his customers. She was a lang, narra-nibbit deam, wi' thin straicht hair, an' a sharp grippit face on her that aye mindit' ye on a soor sweetie. The auld mannies said that Nancy tickled naebody's fancy, least of a' Sandy's.

At last it was your turn. Sandy would plank ye on the stool on the big chair, whip an auld broon cloot roon' yer neck — an' ye were ready.

"Jist a wee trimmie?" he would ask.

"Aye, fine Sandy," ye would reply, "an' mither says tae mak share that there's nae hair left owre ma lugs!"

The comb an' shears would fecht awa', an the outer layer o' yer winter pelt would fa' in little roond twists on the stane flair. Sandy was fell deef an' had a hearin' aid, which would whistle an' toot on, an' maybe send messages tae the gas lichts. It was rare fun tae sit back an' listen tae the high-soun'n schreichs tumlin' oot o' Sandy's artificial lug, an' it rarely failed tae tak yer mind aff the haircut. Jist faun a'thing was goin' fine, Nancy would appear at the door wi' some complaint.

"Ye've forgotten tae tak in coal," she would whine, or rale sharp like, "Faun ye've feenisht that laddie's hair, ye'll jist come richt ben for yer tea!"

The spell o' the journey through space on the wavebands o' Sandy's hearin' aid would be shattered. Sandy would mutter a reply.

"Aye, fine lass." or "Richt ye are, Nancy."

An' if he happened tae be clippin' the back o' yer heid at the time, yer scalp would get a richt yark, which was really meant for Nancy.

At last it was feenisht.

"Cream?" Sandy would inquire, wi' a great hanfu' clorted on tae yer heid afore ye had time tae answer. The comb an' brush plooed oot the white furr o' yer pairtin' , an' if ye warna ready for't — ye got a fair surprise at the billiard ba' lookin' back at ye fae the ither side o' Sandy's mirror. Doon aff yer stool ye gaed an' handit Sandy yer tanner, which went intae the cardboard box that served for a till.

"Fine, laddie, fine!" Sandy would say, tweekin' yer lug. "Stick in at the schule, an' dinna be a barber!"

And, as the hearin' aid whistled ae last farewell, ye escaped intae the sunlicht speckle o' a Spring evenin'.

But Sandy got the last laugh, on a'body. Ae nicht at Taranty Fair, Sandy had a suppie owre muckle, an' fell in wi' a fortune tellin' wifie. She was big, fat and jolly — nae like Nancy ava — an' she fair took a notion o' Sandy, shuttin' her caravan door, an' makin' a richt soss o' him. An' the next mornin', faun the bonnie paintit' caravans were a' awa, Sandy was awa an' a — wi' the show wifie.

An' Nancy's face got aye the soorer.

Ian D. Hendry

The Bursting Boughs of May

In 1924, the year we poached a salmon for the Moderator, there were only five of us: myself aged fifteen, Archie, twelve, Willie ten,

Rona, six and Kenneth, a baby in his cot. John, the youngest had yet to be born.

At the time, as minister of the small country parish of Southend, Kintyre, my father drew an annual stipend which fluctuated on the edge of £350, out of which he had to maintain a Manse with eleven rooms, six dilapidated outhouses and a garden like a park, as well as a hungry family. He had never heard of such a thing as an expense account. In the circumstances, a two-day visit of the Moderator of the Church of Scotland, touring Kintyre in mid-autumn, posed for him an anxious problem. On the administrative side it posed an even more anxious problem for my mother — and for Maimie, the maid.

The Moderator, however, turned out to be a jovial man — he was the Right Rev. David Cathels, DD, of Hawick — who could discuss not only Church law but also other more interesting subjects: fishing and golf, for example, and the Olympic achievements of Eric Liddell. He complimented my mother on her soda scones, and when Rona upset her breakfast milk on his shiny black breeches, his infectious chuckle soon chased away visions of a wrath to come.

At about five o'clock on the second evening, disaster struck. By this time the chickens and eggs supplied by kindly parishoners had all been eaten, but as a special treat for our guest at what we called 'the last supper', my mother had reserved a magnificient cold tongue. For some reason, however, the larder door was left open, and Roy, a yellow collie from the neighbouring farm of Kilblaan, saw his chance and took it. The last anybody saw of the tongue was in Roy's mouth as he disappeared over the garden wall with a flick of his white-tipped tail.

Tears were in my mother's eyes. Though guiltless, for once, Archie and I stood by her, consumed by sympathy. Willie and Rona had gone· to ground beneath gooseberry-bushes in the garden: a prudent move, because Maimie was darting back and forth, scolding everybody.

'Now all we have is tinned salmon!' said my mother. 'Think of it. Tinned salmon for the most important man in Scotland, next to the King!'

My father, always inept in a domestic crisis, muttered a vague

'Dominus providebit', which happens to be the motto of our clan. But Archie and I exchanged looks of inspiration. We went out into the garden and joined Willie and Rona under the gooseberries.

'Listen!' I said, with an eldest brother's authority. 'There's a big salmon in the pool below the bridge: we saw him this morning. If we caught him now, he could be cooked in time for supper.'

'Your rod's broke,' said Rona.

'I've thought of something else. We'll make a landing-net out of the Dutch-hoe, a loop of fence wire and the string net from Kenneth's cot.'

Archie, the honest one, said: 'That'll be poaching.'

'Yes, but it's for the Moderator. He's a holy man, so it's okay.'

Some years later, studying Moral Philosophy at Glasgow University we both detected a flaw in this argument. But at the time it satisfied us; and when our preparations were complete we went into action with no qualms of conscience.

A latter-day Penelope, Rona remained at the Manse to counter awkward questions with guileless words; Archie and Willie took up their positions as scouts, a hundred yards away on either side of the bridge, while I, chewing a handful of gooseberries as a rather frightened gangster might chew gum, crept cautiously to the burn's edge.

I saw him at once in the clear water, brown, red-spotted, sensuously rubbing himself against a boulder. His nose pointed upstream; his tail moved from side to side.

Gripping a bridge support with one hand, I lowered the net with the other. In the evening quiet the only sound was a tinkle from the burn as it flowed steeply into the pool. Scent of newly cut corn mingled with a tarry odour from the bridge.

He saw the net and twitched backwards. I persisted, holding impatience in check. The white string bag moved towards him; eighteen inches, a foot, six inches. My mouth was dry and salty.

Then I decided to stake our plan on one desperate sweep. Tense with anticipation, I thrust the net forward and, as I thrust, suddenly found inside it a furious, fighting twelve pound fish. I tried to heave it up but lost my hold of the bridge support. I slipped and fell and splashed headlong into the water.

A shock of fair hair appeared above me. 'The keeper's coming!' said Archie.

I struggled out of the burn and killed the salmon with a stone. 'Act the decoy!' I ordered. 'Collect Willie and make your way home, round by the church.'

Then, soaked to the skin, I ran like a deer for the slope leading to the Manse. In the end, panting and almost done, but still undetected by the gamekeeper, I staggered into the kitchen and laid our catch at my mother's feet.

I still remember that triumphant evening and the grace my father said as he lifted the cover off the steaming fish: 'Lord, we ask Thy blessing upon these mercies. Accept our thanks and forgive our sins.'

We remember, too, that the Moderator nearly forgot to close his eyes.

From *Salt in My Porridge: Confessions of a Minister's Son*
by Angus MacVicar

Discipline!

As I gaed doon by kirk and toun
I heard the larkies singin,
And ilka burnie treetlin doon,
And wid and welkin ringin.

As I gaed doon by kirk and toun,
Quo I, "A skweel, gweed feth!"
And there I heard nae sang nor soun',
But bairns quaet as death!

J. C. Milne

Parents' Lines and Visits from the Thirties

While the teacher's work brings him mainly into contact with children, he has often a fairly direct relationship with their parents. Almost every morning brings him a few "lines" requesting him to excuse pupils for absence, lateness, or non-preparation of lessons. These are generally quite formal and monotonous, and until recent years they nearly all ended with "and oblidge," with the "d" well to the fore. In general they lend no support to the idea that an earlier crop of scholars (now parents) could write, spell, or compose better that their children do to-day.

I presume that only mistakes of the pen caused one parent to address me as "The Head Waster," and another to request me to "execute John for being away a message."

Spelling and punctuation are serious traps for the unwary parent, and so we learn that "Alex had a sceptic throat," that "Sir William cut his finger," that "John was absent because his mother was washing George Bell," or that "Tom was kept at home because his grandmother died yesterday to oblige his mother."

"Please excuse the bear as she has been away with the brown cats," in spite of its zoological look, was simply a reference to the bearer's bronchitis. A Lanarkshire mother wrote, "Excuse David being absent two days as he was at Hamilton being birched. I have the honour to be, His Mother." A few more lines at random include:

"Please excuse Helen for being absent as she was required at home as the baby was unwell and could not come." (Larkhall).

"I don't think Georgina is fit to get her teeth extracted. She has been a delicate child and forbye I think taking out her teeth would strain her neck and oblidge." (Cullen).

"Dear Teacher, James Fraser has swollen glands and a bad throat. I will get them cut in the summer time."   (Buckie).

"Excuse Jeanie as her face has broken out through her inside."
(Banff).

From the mother of a big strong boy, who had been punished, "His father and I object to anyone touching him. We never hit him at home unless in self- defence."

Under the "lines" from home we must include that vital document the birth certificate. A little Buckie boy was sent home for his birth certificate, to check the particulars regarding him in the register. Having perused it, the teacher gave it back to him. On her way home she found Johnny weeping bitterly on the railway bridge. It was one of those days when the wind sweeps across Buckie at 60 miles an hour. She asked what ailed him. Pointing to a buff paper fluttering far away in the direction of the harbour, he exclaimed, "I've lost ma excuse for being born!"

The parent who courts a "row" with the teacher usually turns up at school, but sometimes she or he takes pen in hand instead, or as a preliminary to her visit.

Here is the exact transcript of a "line" sent by a Stonehouse mother to one of my male teachers: "Mr. — i never thought you would of done to John ear what you have done John is a very thoughtful honest boy and would not tell me a lie he has a very sore ear i fear if i had been in Larkhall instead of Stonehouse i would of let you now more about it i dont sopose he will be back again. You are not a stranger to me so you need not show your power i am shaking just now if i had you heare God help you."

Fortunately or unfortunately, not many teachers are subjected to the same ordeal as a teacher in a mining town in Lanarkshire is reported to have had to face some 50 years ago. It was a time when the miners and the teachers were not on good terms. A new teacher was appointed, fresh from the city. He was warned by others of the "electric" nature of the atmosphere, but, confident in the knowledge that he was a skilled boxer, he was not greatly perturbed. One day he gave a boy a well-deserved thrashing. The father came up that afternoon, and objected, saying truculently, "You wouldn't do it to me!" The unexpected reply was, "I think I could take you on at 4 o'clock." When the school was "skailed" for the day there was quite a crowd outside. "Now," said the teacher, "I have no second to see fair play." Several volunteers at once offered themselves, and they all adjourned to the banks of the Clyde. The teacher had easily the best of the fight, and was loudly cheered at its conclusion. It is even suggested that had the miners been able to influence the Board sufficiently, the Head Teacher might have been deposed in the champion's favour.

Parental visits are not always with a view to making complaints: A Dumfriesshire mother paid a kindly visit to a lady teacher: "I've just come to tell ye ye'll no hiv to dunch Maggie in the back. Ye see, Maggie has a gless e'e. The last teacher gied her a dunch, and oot cam' the e'e, an' doon went the teacher in a faint. So ye'll ken to be careful!"

From *Scottish School Humour* by Charles W. Thomson

Lang Breeks

Well, well, it would be my last crack at Aunt Sally, there was no doubt about that. I had smashed a lot of her clay pipes in my time but this would be the last of it. I can see her twisted old mouth yet, her chalky face and apple-red cheeks, her coconut hair her hat all askew from the whacks she got.

I would be fourteen the day after the school picnic and starting work with Auld Weelum MacKenzie of Fernieden. And besides, I was wearing my father's trousers, and taking a drag on his pipe on the sly. I was getting that big I was beginning to look down my nose at the old man, and I looked ridiculous in knee-length breeks. I had fine sturdy knees and I liked showing them off, but it just wouldn't do any more. I even asked for a kilt, but mother said we couldn't afford it. But I think she was afraid of what the neighbours would say if I swanked about in a kilt, or that it would attract the girls prematurely, and then she'd be jealous.

I could still wear my socks with the coloured tops but nobody would see them under the old man's baggy trousers. First day I appeared in them at school the dominie fair sized me up. He had me out in the middle of the floor and walked round about me with his tongue in his cheek. I knew he wanted to take me down to size and making a fool of me in front of the class was one way of doing it.

He never did like me that dominie. I was always late and often absent and always seemed to rub him up the wrong way.

But my long trousers fair needled him. "I'll take you on ten years after this," he said, his toothbrush moustache bristling red, "If you would only come to school man, maybe I could make something of you. You have the makings of a scholar but you are a truant lout. You should be thrashed! Maybe your father isn't big enough to do it but God I am. Get back to your seat and sit very quietly or I'll really get mad."

I ran on the old man's bicycle, smoked his pipe, wore his Sunday sark, threw stones, fired arrows, kissed the girls — what was the old man to do?

And damnit he was glad of me too. He was chauved to death in the byres and I ran home from school and sliced his turnips, carried straw, swept up; I even took his place for a fortnight when he was off with 'flu, so he could hardly hit a lad that did that for him — well, not often.

But I had talent that the old man couldn't see; gifts that might have landed him on easy street had he given me some encouragement. I was publishing my own monthly magazine of short stories (hand-written, of course) and sending them round the parish. I had begun a history of Roman Britain with illustrations that might have rivalled Gibbon's 'Decline and Fall.' I was coming on as a strip cartoonist and poster artist and even the dominie had allowed me to design and paint covers for the annual school magazines. He asked for a show of hands in my favour and it was unanimous.

I had the most unique puppet-theatre you ever heard of, all done with silhouettes and a wick lamp on a life-size screen; on-coming trains, stunting aeroplanes, ships at sea, sword fights, bathing beauties — the lot, and the neighbours used to give me threepence a time for a peep-show.

I built model herring drifters that floated on the miller's dam. I made a motor-coach, a binder, and a merry-go-round with swing chairs and painted ladies on the revolving panels. I could make almost anything from cardboard, a handful of pins and water colours. I had to because nobody could afford to give me toys. Anyway, I didn't want a mecanno set or a fretwork outfit because that was someone else's ideas. I wanted to be original and invent my own playthings. But a magic lantern at this stage would have been a real blessing.

I had a standing army of one hundred soldiers, every one a cardboard cut-out equipped and decorated with pencil and paint brush, even Highlanders in kilts. Sometimes I had a war, when I opened up on them with my pea-cannon, and the side left with most troops upright were the victors, and I coloured another part of the map red for a British victory, green, mauve or purple for an imaginary foe.

What could the dominie teach me anyway? Algebra? Mathematics? A dreary lot, subjects that probably I would never have need for, not even as a mental exercise 'cause I had plenty of that.

The dominie bored me and I disliked the brute. I had far more important things to learn than he could teach me. I was mad about Halley's Comet for instance and he never even mentioned the Solar System. And anyway when he asked the class a question I had my hand up first. And I could sketch a rough map of the world without a copy. I had read most of the books in the J. & P. Coates library. The dominie even gave me a prize for general knowledge, second for gardening — gardening, heavens!

But nothing short of an earthquake or a tidal wave could get me up in the morning. I had to run all of three miles to school on a 'jammy piece,' through wet fields and over the moor, my books in a bundle under my arm, sometimes my slate when home to be scrubbed, never a moment to spare.

The only morning I got up early was to watch the total eclipse of the sun. I was up at six with my father to get it on show for my newsreel — a device I used that William Friese-Green would have shook my hand for.

I might have been a Walt Disney, a Beaverbrook, a Sam Goldwyn, a Bernard Shaw — but the old man had never heard of these men. They were only shadows, he said; they had no substance, they existed only on paper — never make a living that way lad.

The only people the old man knew were those that slaved their guts out for the neighbouring farmers. He could see these men, he could talk to them, he didn't have to go boring his head into books to find out what they had to say. He lived in a narrow world the old man and he couldn't read a book anyway, nor even write his name, or count his pay, not without mother looking over his shoulder to see that it was right.

Somebody said to the old man that that loon o' his could be on the stage yet. "Him on the stage!" said the old man, "none o' that for him; I had tae work afore his day and he'll hae tae dee the same. Na, na, he's nae gaun tae loaf aboot idle when he leaves the skweel!"

I don't blame the old man really but that was his philosophy. And when I started sending my stories to an editor and they came right back he really had me licked.

"Niver mak' money that wye ma loon, nae wi' a pincil ahin yer lug — wark is the only sure wye tae mak' a livin'; ye'll jist hae tae wark like the rest o' us."

Maybe I could make my own way in the world. But what could I do without money, without influence, in my old man's trousers? And for once he had the old woman on his side. She didn't understand me either but I couldn't leave her, not without her blessing anyway.

Nobody understood me or cared — and why should they? I was such an eccentric oddity, neurotic almost.

But there was still Auntie Sally and the school picnic. And there was this job with Auld Weelum MacKenzie of Fernieden. So I gets up on my toes and looks straight down my blower at the old man, real stern like, to make him look like a twirp, and I tells him flat I'm not going to work on the farms. It was a cheek I know, but a fellow has to put his foot down, even if he tramples his own toes in the process.

From *Straw into Gold* by David Toulmin

A dominie's say

Dod Gordon left baith skweel and beuck
Te wark his faither's butchin heuck,
And noo he's bocht gweed Gushetneuk
And Kittlenyackit!
But me, wi' a' my learnin-look
At my teem backit!

O sair I vrocht wi' Jock McGhee,
Te pit him through his H.L.C!
And noo a dental surgeon-he!
In his fite jaicket!
Wi' mebbe fower times mair than me,
And weel respeckit!

Syne look at Gabblin Jamie Broon!
A teem, lang-leggit, glaiket loon,
Wha'd nivver worn a college goon,
Na, but for me!
And noo they ca' him Doctor Broon,
An LL.D!

It's nae yer learnin nor yer lear
That mak's a man respeckit here!
But reemin routh o' warldly gear,
— The mair's the pity! —
Or gift o' gab te mak' a steer
Fae Cults te Fitty!

O Learnin, hide yer peer, fite face
Ahin the sacrist's shinin mace!
For deevil's chance or want o' grace,
—I dinna ken—
Gars mony an ablach win the race
Owre better men!

J.C. Milne

The Hinmaist Thocht

Gin I was God

Gin I was God, sittin' up there abeen,
Weariet nae doot noo a' my darg was deen,
Deaved wi' the harps an' hymns oonendin' ringin',
Tired o' the flockin' angels hairse wi' singin',
To some clood-edge I'd daunder furth an', feth,
Look ower an' watch hoo things were gyaun aneth.
Syne, gin I saw hoo men I'd made mysel'
Had startit in to pooshan, sheet an' fell,
To reive an' rape, an' fairly mak' a hell
O' my braw birlin' Earth, — a hale week's wark—
I'd cast my coat again, rowe up my sark,
An', or they'd time to lench a second ark,
Tak' back my word an' sen' anither spate,
Droon oot the hale hypothec, dicht the sklate,
Own my mistak', an', aince I'd cleared the brod,
Start a'thing ower again, gin I was God.

Charles Murray